DISCLOSURE OF CORPORATE SOCIAL PERFORMANCE

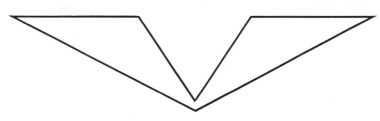

Survey, Evaluation, and Prospects

Harold L. Johnson

T0123908

PRAEGER PUBLISHERS
Praeger Special Studies

New York • London • Sydney • Toronto

Library of Congress Cataloging in Publication Data

Johnson, Harold L
   Disclosure of corporate social performance.

   Bibligoraphy: p.
   Includes index.
   1. Industry--Social aspects--United States.
I. Title.
HD60.5.U5J66   658.4'08   78-10594
ISBN 0-03-047206-7

PRAEGER PUBLISHERS
PRAEGER SPECIAL STUDIES
383 Madison Avenue, New York, N.Y. 10017, U.S.A.

Published in the United States of America in 1979
by Praeger Publishers,
A Division of Holt, Rinehart and Winston, CBS, Inc.

9   038   987654321

ACKNOWLEDGMENTS

This project, supported by the research committee of the Emory Business School, was worked on both in Atlanta, Georgia and Cuchara, Colorado; the major effort completed in Colorado. Russell Morrison, my research assistant at Emory, made a significant contribution in bringing together the materials for my analysis. Elizabeth Millerman, a dear Cuchara friend, made valuable editorial suggestions, once the manuscript was completed. To the research committee and to these individuals, I owe gratitude and appreciation.

'79- 2188

CONTENTS

LIST OF TABLES AND FIGURES

Disclosure of
Corporate
Social Performance

1

INTRODUCTION

The topic of corporate social reporting has ramifications far beyond technical issues of interest only to public accountants and corporate controllers. Actually, its importance is apparent in the intensity of discussion in some of the literature, an intensity that belies any notion of experts debating procedural niceties. Indeed, the topic raises important questions about the role, range, and function of accounting in contemporary society that are guaranteed to excite competing philosophies and views of accounting.

More important, however, corporate social reporting leads to serious implications and controversy as to the nature of evolving contemporary capitalism. It directly implies institutional adjustments in the structure and process of the market economy. The import of an evolving capitalism lends the subject of corporate social reporting a certain public significance. Some see it as meaning a stronger enterprise system confronting many of its current disabilities, while others argue that it denotes a decaying market order sliding toward socialism. One thing is certain about the ambiguous and confusing developments in corporate social reporting or accounting. A full-blown system of social accounting involves institutional change both within the firm as well as in the larger context of the U.S. economic system.

Corporate social reporting (hereafter referred to as CSR) has generated work and discussion from a wide variety of researchers and practitioners. As might be expected, accountants with corporations, CPA firms, and in academe have been actively involved in the area. However, law professors, economists, business executives, management science scholars, management professors, consultants, and activists in the movement for corporate reform have all contributed to the exploding literature and practice on CSR. A diverse set of theoreticians and practitioners is at work in the field.

While the subject is one of considerable social significance, in some respects it is a new development on the business agenda. It has attracted attention and interest essentially from the late 1960s to the present. Yet the burgeoning literature and activities of the past decade do allow us to isolate the major trends and issues, to evalute models, and to forecast what the future likely holds. Periodic "state of the art" assessments have been made in the past few years, but the expanding pace of work in the field demands frequent reassessments. There clearly has been an accelerating ferment and development in CSR since 1970.

Before we address the substance, significance, and controversy of CSR, it is useful to briefly anticipate the focus and conclusions of this book. For better or for worse, large U.S. corporations are going to be in the business of corporate social reporting or disclosure. It is not merely a fad that will die down as attention is directed to other issues. The trend and pressure is toward expansion of CSR. Efforts of corporate teams and scholarly researchers in the past few years have pushed the matter well "up the learning curve," to use one of the well-worn cliches of the field, so that second-generation CSR schemes are likely to materialize.

The commonplace image of the partially filled container aptly illustrates the current status of CSR. Part of what is seen relates to some kind of personal pessimism/optimism index. Some critics are quite disappointed in the practical results of all the sound and fury that has accompanied CSR, while enthusiastic observers see marked progress at this stage. Clearly the developmental stage of CSR has not fulfilled the promise of its greatest supporters. Formidable conceptual obstacles remain, and the nuts and bolts of measurement tools are only slowly being assembled; political and administrative challenges within the enterprise are serious. Yet in a few years sharp advances have been made; the domain of CSR has now been clarified, and its major elements have been identified. The container looks half full.

Part of what is seen in such an ambiguous, complex subject also depends upon the kind of methodological or paradigmatic lens focused upon it. As will be discussed in a moment, analysts who enter the discussion with the perspective of standard, neoclassical economics view CSR with considerable alarm and skepticism. They see either deterioration in the profit focus of market-oriented enterprises—or pure hogwash. On the other hand, if the paradigmatic lens is that of an institutional, organizational, or social economics, the appraisal is much more favorable.

The perspective of this analysis is taken from the latter stance; it sees a strengthening of the market system as corporations more fully achieve the socioeconomic agenda demanded by the American people. It strengthens rather than destroys by building social control through disclosure rather than heavy-handed regulation.

2

SOCIAL RESPONSIBILITY
AND CSR CLARIFIED

The discussion and debates of the past decade have left current research on CSR with a long list of provocative questions and dilemmas. But despite numerous unresolved difficulties, researchers nonetheless have successfully generated many relatively firm conclusions. The dust of exploration has settled enough so that at least some answers to fundamental questions are available. It is the epitome of wasted effort for CSR critics and supporters to wrestle, as some are wont to do, with issues that have been set to rest in well-founded and broadly recognized discussions. The task here is to survey the essentially established conclusions that have been reached in recent analyses and investigations, with the aim of encouraging work to move on to new ground. Our preliminary task will be to sort out what is already known.

Before elaborating on these conclusions, however, it may be useful to clarify the terminology. Exactly what are we talking about? Social *reports*, social *accounting*, or social *audits*? Opinion in the field is divided over the use of these terms; each designation has its advocates and detractors. Accountants apparently prefer the term "social accounting," criticizing the idea of social audits. Independent attestation of data or procedures is not as yet a part of the game except in isolated instances. The common denominator, both in scholarly treatises and in actual practice, however, is that of corporate reports on social performance beyond that implied in traditional financial data. The reports are either essentially in-house—for management perusal and action—or published externally for a variety of audiences.

A number of efforts are under way to systemize the collection and dissemination of nonfinancial information in forms reminiscent of traditional financial documents. As this work is perfected, the phrase "corporate social accounting" will have an increasing validity in correctly designating what is going on. Corporate social accounting in the sense of the structuring and presentation of crucial information holds exciting potential for business. At the present moment significant research in this conceptual innovation is well under way, as will be described later.

At this point, though, it is a case of the wish being father to the thought, or of an overinterpretation of current findings to conclude that full-blown social accounting is already an established field safe from serious attack. Independent attestation in an auditing of accounting results as an established practice lies on an even more distant horizon. At this stage only social reporting, albeit generally faulty, incomplete, and without any accounting rationale and certification, is the accomplished fact of corporate disclosure. Thus, having eliminated the alternatives, the CSR designation remains the proposed nomenclature.

A SOCIAL ECONOMICS PARADIGM
OF BUSINESS/SOCIETY INTERPLAYS

The terms "measurement and disclosure of corporate social performance" and "corporate social responsibility" indicate the close connection between these phenomena. Actually, the relationship is one of cause and effect, for the requirements of social responsibility create pressure for reporting on business behavior associated with these social requisites. Social responsibility is thus intrinsically linked with CSR. The fundamental idea of social responsibility has been clarified and rigorously defined in inquiries of recent years. Lengthy though it may be, definition does pay off in a firm understanding of the *role* and *content* of corporate social reporting.

The controversy over social responsibility arises due to alternative perceptions of the nature of economic or business reality. A core issue in this reality, which these conceptual maps or frameworks focus upon is the linkage between the business firm and its context of operation. How are the business firm and the external world connected? There are two conceptual frameworks for exploring the nature of this linkage, standard, neoclassical economics and institutional, social economics. An examination of these two comprehensions of business reality goes to the heart of the disputes over the nature of social responsibility.

The conceptual map of conventional, neoclassical economics, undoubtedly the dominant paradigm in many circles, conceives of linkages between the enterprise and its environment largely in terms of market transactions. The firm or corporation is connected through multitudinous quid pro quo ties of trade, exchange, and contract with that environment. Of course, users of this perceptual mode also recognize that markets operate in contexts of law, custom, and ethics, but this recognition is quickly superceded by an almost complete concentration on theoretically pure markets, prices, and profits. Within this paradigmatic framework, social responsibility is seen as an altruistic aberration as the self-aggrandizement of managers of monopoly enterprises. Alternatively, it is a public relations ploy of sophisticated business interests seeking political support from the American citizenry. In sum, it is either a fraud or the sign of dangerous deterioration in market institutions.

This brief sketch should suffice to capture the flavor of this conceptual map. It is the familiar paradigm of elementary microeconomics. It is a sophisti-

cated yet simple demonstration of how the market system as an instrument of informal social control transforms the pursuit of self-interest into social benefit in
the mode of Adam Smith.

The alternative conceptual framework of social economics perceives business enterprises as acting within a larger social system than that of market transactions, with all suprasystem elements complexly interdependent.* This understanding of social reality organized in a structure of mutual interaction and impact
is an expansion of the input-output economic model of Wassily Leontief, the No-
bel prize-winning economist who singlehandedly developed this mode of analysis.

An illustration of this paradigmatic insight into socioeconomic interdependence is depicted in Figures 2.1 and 2.2. Figure 2.2 is a disaggregation of the econ-
omy/economy cell of the larger matrix, showing as firms, unions, and government,
some of the economy participants. To read this model following the structure of
the Leontief economic model, each sector of society, such as education, health,
or business, has impacts on or outputs to other elements of the system; these impacts and outputs are shown in the applicable row of the figure. Each sector, on
the other hand, receives a rich array of inputs from other elements of society;
these inputs are reflected in each column of the matrix. Figures 2.1 and 2.2 are
"empty" in the sense that the particulars of interdependence are not shown;
rather their intent is to illustrate the primary fact of interplay among sectors of
society in a broader system than that portrayed in conventional microeconomics.

As a point of interest, standard economics is concerned only with *intrasec-
toral* interchanges within the economy/economy confluence in Figures 2.1 and
2.2. The conceptual map of social economics, on the other hand, *explicitly* wid-
ens the purview of economics to include at least some of the complex interchanges between the business system and other elements of society, as shall be
seen shortly. A myopic focus on the economic dimensions of the broad socioeconomic matrix alone may be useful in economic analysis for certain technical purposes, but it is disastrous in terms of truly comprehending the nature of the linkage between the firm and its total environment. It leads to what might be called
the Friedman Misconception, that is, the view that the enterprise is altogether
and solely an economic organization, divorced from its sociocultural setting.†

To give some content to this matrix, a fundamental input to business firms
from the remainder of the social system is a set of socioeconomic performance
criteria to be achieved as economic activity takes place. These socioeconomic
goals or criteria can be categorized in various ways, but the following lists the
main elements: a high and growing GNP (perhaps refined to a GNP net of exces-

---

*This analytical framework has an illustrious intellectual history in the contributions
of Thorstein Veblen, John Maurice Clark, Wesley Mitchell, Adolph Berle, and John R. Com-
mons.

†This misconception is identified with Milton Friedman in recognition of the fact that
his adherence to the standard economics paradigm has made him a principle critic of the social responsibility concept. Of course, many others fall into the error of the Friedman Misconception.

FIGURE 2.1

The Multisector Socioeconomic Input-Output Model

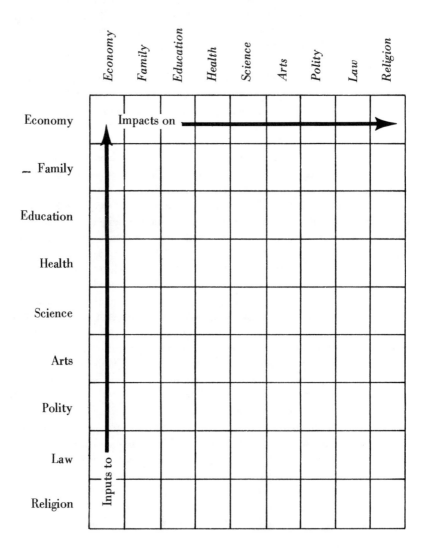

Source: Joseph S. Berliner, *Economy, Society and Welfare: A Study in Social Economics* (New York: Praeger, 1972), p. 32.

FIGURE 2.2

The Economy Sector of the Input-Output Model

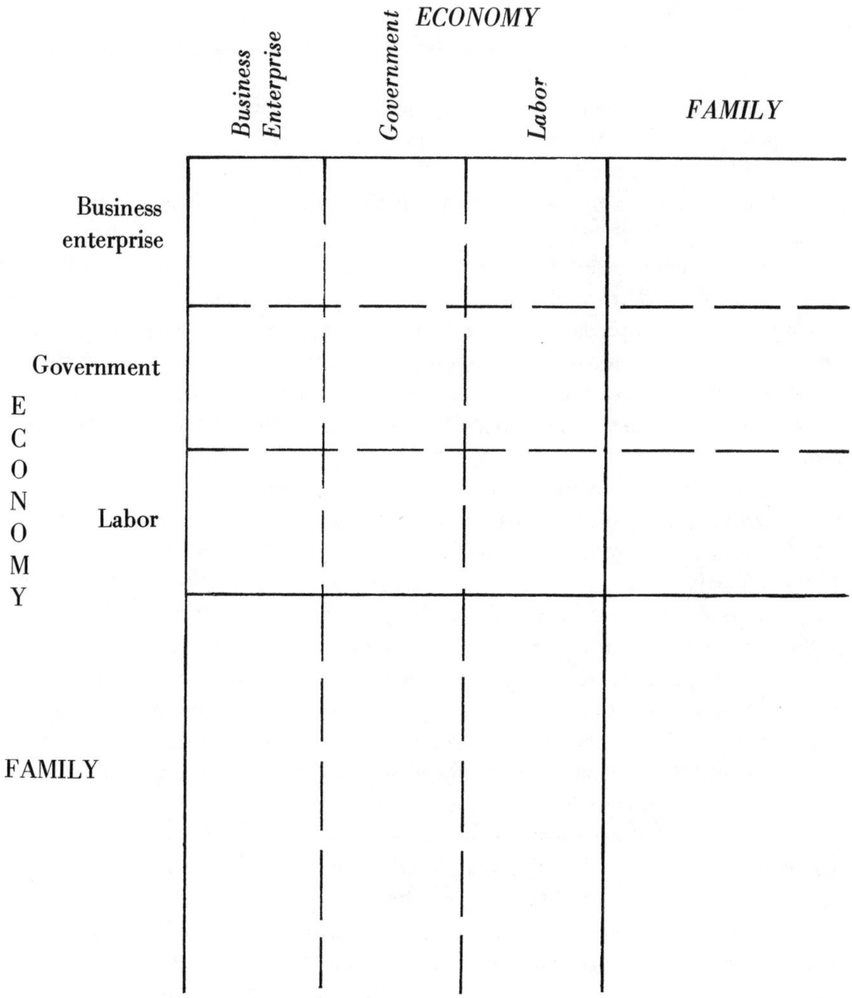

Source: Compiled by the author.

sive pollution, urban disamenities, and other discommodities of modern life), economic stability, efficiency, justice, freedom, security, and an economy in which honorable individuals of personal integrity can achieve their income aspirations.[1] These goals are a reasonable facsimile of the broad yardstick by which economic performance is measured in contemporary American society.

Another input element to the economy from the rest of society is that of a normative order that sets out in a detailed range of prescriptions how business is to be conducted. The norms of business prescribe behavior over a gamut of activity, ranging from how plants are to be closed, workers laid off, and consumers and suppliers treated, spelling out the details of supervisor-worker relations, the quality of physical working conditions, the content of fringe benefits, and the style of sales efforts. This is only a partial listing of normative business requirements.

The normative order is incorporated into the thoughts and actions of American citizens through a socialization process that starts with childhood and continues in the social groupings of clubs, religious organizations, professional bodies, and schools. Not all individuals are genuine adherents to all norms—where they are at the level of conscience. Many accept the normative signals of society because they realize sanctions and penalties associated with violations of behavioral requisites.

As important elements in the context of economic activity, performance criteria and the normative order become part of an informal social control process for business behavior analogous to informal control via the market system. Both are partly unconscious, tacit coordinators of action, and both transform private into public interests only imperfectly. Very few people wish to rely altogether on the market or on norms as instruments of social control.

One insight of social-economics' conceptual map is that all economies are traditional systems with social requisites for economic behavior. It is not only Stone Age tribes or the peoples of eighteenth century India that can be characterized as traditional economies. Traditional economies are universal in the sense that economic life inevitably takes place within a matrix of social goals, values, and norms. Consumers choose goods and services, and entrepreneurs seek profits; but they do so in a social setting that greatly affects the choices made. In simple terms, it is just a figment of the analyst's imagination to conceive of *pure* economies or business action independent of a sociocultural context. The social context *prescribes* performance criteria and norms, and executives forget them at their corporation's peril. Sanctions of labor unrest, government regulation, consumer agitation, cessation of purchases, and, as we shall see shortly, lower profits, are the socioeconomic system's mechanisms for policing the enterprise system. The policing goes on *through* as well as outside market transactions.

Some recognition of this conclusion by standard economists is apparent in their frequent reference to business or market behavior within the "rules of the game." This phrase is generally taken to mean the laws, court decisions, and bureaucratic regulations of a contemporary economy. However, the emphasis here is on the important understanding that the phrase also encompasses the goals or socioeconomic performance criteria, normative expectations, and ethics or *ethos* of a society. These along with the earlier list are key elements in the instructions to the various players in the game. To describe all economies as traditional is to state that economic activity takes place within constraints of particular "rules of the game" as described here. Rules of the game are universal; that is, they are found in all economies.

One significant contribution of social economics' conception of business reality is the awareness that enterprises are judged by a complex, evolving, and partly competing set of performance yardsticks that involve more than profits, efficiency, and the outpouring of goods and services. Thus, one way of understanding corporate social reporting is to see it as including disclosure of information, which relates to such social goals as economic justice, stability, and freedom.

THE FIRM AS COALITION

Debate about social responsibility is also fueled by alternative conceptions of the business firm. These different views are perhaps related to the preceding conceptual maps, but they offer additional clues about the nature of social responsibility and the content of CSR. These opposing analytical perceptions are the traditional economic-legal view and the organization theory construction elaborated largely by scholars associated with Carnegie-Mellon University. Richard Cyert and James March are two leading developers of the latter image of the firm.

According to the traditional framework, the enterprise is concentrated in the role and goals of the entrepreneur who contracts with owners of various inputs for their services and commodities into the production process. The objective function of the firm is solely that of the entrepreneur who, particularly in competitive markets, is motivated by a single-minded focus on profits. Owners of inputs are said to take up the purpose of the entrepreneur as part of a contractual quid pro quo, for it is the entrepreneur's commercial venture, not theirs. If workers dislike their jobs, if consumers are dissatisfied with the quality or safety of products, or if dealers are outraged by arbitrary treatment—they vote with their feet, departing the relationship in search of greener pastures.

By traditional legal understandings, stockholders in the corporation perform the entrepreneural function, with executives acting simply as the owners' agents. Managerial duties of loyalty and care basically mean making as much profit as possible for the stockholders. Stewardship responsibilities of executives extend only to the pecuniary interests of corporate shareholders.

As might be expected, the organization theory perception of the enterprise stands in sharp opposition to this depiction. The firm is conceived of as a shifting coalition of participants in the production process, each member coming with considerations to be gratified in the corporate relationship. The firm is not the entrepreneur; it is a mix or coalition that includes executives, employees, dealers, suppliers, and stockholders, all of whom are held together by the expectation that at least minimum requisites for participation will be obtained out of the fluctuating relationships. Each participant wants "his own thing" from the organization, a package of monetary and nonmonetary results.

In the organization theory image, the large U.S. corporation is indeed a public institution, partly because its shareholders number into the hundreds of thousands. But it is public, most emphatically, with its membership expanded to include a diverse coalition of interests; the number of individuals who both influence and who are influenced by the behavior of the corporation is great.

As a possible criticism, it should be noted that surely all of the myriad of the corporation's participants are not equally excited about its policies and behavior. Many consumers and employees, for example, are associated only by relatively tenuous links of contract, credit, or cash rather than in significant negotiation concerning specific company policies. This judgment can be countered by the elementary dictum of market economics that all workers or customers need not shift from a market to move prices or wages. Only marginal numbers of market players moving in and out of interchange are sufficient to move prices up or down. As an illustrationof this, all of General Motors' shareholders do not need to sell their shares to generate a significant decline in stock prices. Similarly, it is not necessary that all members of corporate coalitions be equally agitated or powerful in order to influence these large institutions' goals and behavior.

With the corporation as a broad coalition, its goals are thus multiple rather than single. Furthermore, attention is shifted from goal to goal. A simultaneous optimization of multiple objectives as in the allocation decision rule of conventional economic theory does not characterize firm behavior. The objectives of the organization specified by the participating coalition members are addressed one or a few at a time as poor performance with employee safety, shareholder profits, or consumer interest in quick settlement of complaints triggers attention to a particular goal. The analogy is that of a fire engine first moving to one goal failure area and concentrating on it for a time and then being pulled in another direction.

The Carnegie-Mellon model bolstered by nearly two decades of analytical empirical testing is obviously more complex than the few comments of this sketch. However, these are the singular aspects germane to this discussion of social responsibility and CSR. This conception suggests that social responsibility involves at least minimal achievement of the purposes of the employees, stockholders, dealers, executives, and suppliers joined in the organization. Employee interest in safe, healthful work environments come under the rubric of responsibility, as does a certain degree of job security.

This emphasis upon players in the corporate game in addition to stockholders does not necessarily contradict the attention directed to what appear to be more socially oriented performance criteria. Some participants in the corporation can be construed as beneficiaries, custodians, and policers of specific socioeconomic goals. General social yardsticks are given a specificity in the requirements and interests of particular individuals in the enterprise.

For example, economic justice, at first blush a very vague idea, translates readily to less discrimination in employment. Female and minority employees can be counted on to read into the unclear idea of justice very precise aspirations in their particular coalition circumstances. They want more money and equal chances at job training and promotion up the corporate ladder. As another example, due process is the specificity given the general performance criteria of economic freedom as dealers have sought to insulate themselves in various ways from arbitrary treatment by manufacturers. Instead of quietly exiting from corporate coalitions that fall short of their individual goal requirements, dealers have sought to shape the policies and structures of the corporation through negotiation and political power. So it is in the context of participant objectives within the corporation that at least some of the socioeconomic performance criteria are given precise meaning.

An especial relevance to CSR of the organization theory image of the enterprise is that it gives a kind of analytical legitimacy to the idea of diverse constituencies in the corporation. The literature and practice of CSR, as well as of social responsibility, makes constant reference to "constituencies" of the corporation, embracing all of the obvious interest groups associated with an enterprise. It is a mode of expression counter to the often vehement contention that the corporation is solely its entrepreneurial stockholder core. While the organization theory model does not use the politically colored term "constituency," it does underscore the proposition that corporate enterprises are combinations of interest groups seeking diverse objectives from organizational coalitions.

Thus, the idea of constituencies need not be thought of as a figment of public relations hyperbole whereby business managers hope to muster public approval. That, indeed, may be part of it, but this conceptual approach to corporate life gives a social science substance to the conclusion that the corporation may mean more than shareholders.

Additionally, this conception of the corporation communicates the idea that CSR is not directed at an amorphous, perhaps nonexistent, conglomeration called the public. As social responsibility is given at least partial meaning in the interests of employees, consumers, and suppliers, so CSR involves disclosure of information relevant to the objectives of various members of the coalitions that are the United States' large corporations.

THE ENTERPRISE AS CORNUCOPIA

There is a final piece of the puzzle called social responsibility that will improve our understanding of this concept so fundamental to the nature of CSR.

One organizing principle that can be applied to the extraordinarily complex reality of interdependence shown in the socioeconomic input/output model of Figures 2.1 and 2.2 comes from the analytical contributions of Talcott Parsons and Neil Smelser, two leading social scientists. [2] They propose a theoretical framework that suggests how the multisectors of a complicated social system are interrelated. It is a perspective that can be utilized to explore the social function of business and hence give additional insight to the meaning and nature of social responsibility.

According to these investigators, every social system, which can be any group of interacting individuals, from the family through the firm to the entire society, has four basic problems to solve in order to continue to exist. First, each system possesses a value structure and must maintain that structure. Second, a system must attain those values it sets forth. Third, a system must be able to adapt, particularly when a wide variety of system goals must be achieved. In these cases, the system must have the capacity to use its resources to assist in attaining its goals. Finally, the system must integrate all its subparts so that they support and complement each other.

Various subsystems perform each of these functions. The family, religious bodies, television, school, and government are part of the U.S. goal-defining, goal-attaining, and integrational apparatus. For the community-at-large the economy carries out the adaptive function, producing a stream of goods and services that enable society to accomplish its goals. U.S. society, for example, requires a tremendous quantity and variety of goods and services, from electric power plants to fresh frozen beans. By making this flow of goods available, the economy gives the community the power to adapt to events and to attain goals ranging from national defense to Saturday afternoon recreation.

In the societal subsystem called the U.S. economy, the business firm is the principal operating unit. Thus, according to the Parsons-Smelser model, the firm's primary social function is to produce and make innovations in goods and services. By turning out an extraordinary array of goods and services, businesses are carrying out a process essential to social existence. It is the technological delivery apparatus of the social system that, through the generation of goods and services, enables individuals, groups, and the entire society to achieve their respective goals. Some individuals have a vision of a utopia in which society would return to a more primitive, Thoreau-like existence, and one of the virtues of a free society is that those who desire it can pursue this way of life. The main thrust of Western civilization, however, has been to improve society's adaptive capacity and standard of living by increasing output.

This framework of institutional specialization implies that a business operates as a production machine, leaving other social function to other organizations and institutions. However, this is a rather simplistic, though largely correct, injunction. Business firms exist within society and take on some responsibility for society's other three functions: goal attainment, value maintenance, and system integration. Even though its prime role is to produce goods and services, it is at the same time required to help meet other social goals and to facilitate the cohesion of society. Business firms perform such functions when they participate in programs ranging from United Appeal donations to worker recruitment from the ghetto poor. Despite these general requirements, however, the business enterprise is neither a charitable institution, a public school, nor a church or synagogue; its principal social function is to serve as a production machine.

In the vocabulary of Parsons-Smelser, business enterprises are *collectivities,* that is, hybrid organizations associated primarily with one subsystem of society but nonetheless in interchange with other subsystems. The latter linkages color and channel the primary adaptive role of generating gross national product. Raymond Bauer, an important researcher in corporate social reporting, uses similar language to describe the same phenomena.[3] He describes business enterprises as operating in a complex environmental system that can be thought of as having two elements, a task environment and a value-giving environment. The latter defines norms and values and also establishes and enforces society's priorities. In the setting of markets and technology the social task of the business firm is to turn out these necessary groceries," so to speak, that is, the vast array of goods and services thought by consumers to be useful to contemporary existence. Social responsibility thus explicitly and most importantly means the output of product that adds to individual and social capacities and satisfies human desires.

Too many investigators forget the rest of the story though. Economic organizations are embedded in a value-giving environment or are linked in input-output relationships with other subsystems of family, church, government, and school; so the enterprise role and the content of responsibility implies more than production. Nonetheless, this way of deciphering social reality directly implies that corporate social reporting includes such information as the economic task of the enterprise, its productivity record, and the serviceability of its products. This latter, admittedly broad characterization of economic responsibility surely has enough specificity to exclude dangerous, polluting goods, or those sold by deception or fraud.

As a quick summary of this discussion, one dimension of social responsibility is the corporation's attainment of relevant socioeconomic performance standards specified in the normative order of American society. Another dimension includes attention directed to the interests of the diverse coalition members comprising the U.S. corporation. Social responsibility relates to economic justice, stability, and freedom as these goals apply to the requisites of coalition members. A large component of responsibility also includes, as the socioeconomic goal of rising GNP indicates, the output of the multitudinous goods and services necessary for physical and social existence in the modern world. A temporary electric power blackout, an OPEC boycott, or a national transportation strike underscore just how crucial the economic process, the prime domain of business, is to human existence.

CSR consequently includes disclosure of information pertaining to performance criteria not usually addressed in financial statements as well as data on the state of affairs relevant to coalition or constituency expectations. Consumer information about product quality, warranties, and safety and economic facts about productivity, labor relations, and capital expansion are relevant elements as well.

SOCIAL RESPONSIBILITY: WHAT IT ISN'T

This outline tells what social responsibility—and by extension CSR—encompasses. Given the investigations of recent years, it is also useful, however, to examine *what it does not mean*. A variety of false trails, red herrings, and confusions have complicated the discussion of business in the contemporary United States. The first such confusion is that social responsibility gives business managers a portfolio to decide for themselves what constitutes proper behavior. The fear is that executives will decide independently how stockholders' money is to be spent on various "worthy" causes that gratify the tastes and preferences of top managerial officers. As powerful executives frame what business should and should not do, they take on a political role in a free society. A nightmare conjured up is that of nonelected, essentially autocratic but perhaps benevolent, despots allocating resources outside both market and government control. Big business managers are in the saddle with social responsibility.

As a rebuttal to this serious contention, it is useful to recall that in competitive markets, business firms do essentially as they are told. A flow of instructions from consumers signaled by rising and falling profits direct executives' decisions. Similarly, with the informal control of norms and social expectations, executives are given rather explicit directions regarding business behavior. Society rather than freewheeling business writes the prescription for social responsibility. For example, virtually any adult American who ponders the problem for a moment can specify the required parameters of a contemporary employee layoff policy. Those requisites for a responsible personnel policy if dismissed as nonsense would undoubtedly result in lower productivity, deteriorating morale, and future recruitment difficulties.

Instead of being built on the style of powerful organizations taking over the role of government, U.S. corporations are more likely constructed in another way. A thoughtful commentator has used the graphic analogy of a Japanese wrestler, characterizing large corporations as "immense but flabby and easily set quivering by a public relations panic."[4] The behavior of large corporations as illustrated by the election of blacks and women to boards of directors, the institution of administrative structures and telephone hot lines to handle consumer complaints, or contributions to local educational and social service institutions does not appear to be that of managers operating *outside* social expectations.

Instructions to executives that coordinate and direct behavior derive from the tacit control device of markets. Most efforts at telling consumers how they should spend their money, apart from a few oligopoly markets heavily enforced with massive advertising budgets, end up in the shambles of bankruptcy suits. The debacle of bankrupt cluster housing projects all over the country is a case in point when promoters and experts attempted to tell prospective purchasers how the nation's housing problem "should" be solved. In ways similar to the market, the informal controls of norms, values, and social expectations limit and channel business decisions into particular avenues. Costly employee turnover, undesired legislation, antidiscrimination suits, and the rise of the consumer movement are the consequences of executives trying to develop their own definitions of responsible business practice. Responsible executives, as those at the mercy of an effective market apparatus, are more like pawns than despots.

Another false trail toward understanding the nature of social responsibility is to identify it as altruism. This erroneous identification confines social responsibility to a minor fringe of corporate resource allocation, for company contributions total about only 1 or 2 percent of the before-profits taxes of most business organizations. In this picture the whole focus of responsibility and hence of CSR is on the relative minutiae of corporate charity. To be sure, it is excessively naive to suppose that the utility functions of executives are limited to their personal income or wealth, or by some magic of altruism restricted to the income or wealth of stockholders. But the whole intent of the current knowledge of social responsibility is to put it on a basis other than the voluntary expression of goodwill. Social responsibility is a social control on business behavior that prescribes details for all aspects of commercial life, from plant location, capital expansion, marketing, and personnel practice to production and finance.

To characterize responsibility as simply voluntary, altruistic decision making leads the discussion into a morass of confusion about motivation. Does it matter whether an activity is triggered by a component of the objective function, that is, an element of personal goals and motivations, or is prompted by social constraints shaping decisions to certain consequences? Is a particular act carried out because it is genuinely sought or because the sanctions of norms and expectations make it the prudent, expedient decision? The safest answer in looking at many business actions is to conclude that both dimensions are present.* In any event the result is the same whether either aspect has been the cause.

---

*There is at least one piece of empirical evidence that business motivations are a mixture. In a multiple regression analysis of corporate philanthropic contributions, R. A. Schwartz found a "price" elasticity of such contributions arising from changing tax rates was greater than /1/, ranging from /1.06/ to /2.00/ for particular industrial groupings. This is a strong indication that corporate donations are not simply profit motivated, for as tax rates increase by 10 percent, for example, why increase contributions by 15 or 20 percent if profits are the sole goal? That would be overly generous from a pure profit consideration— and that is exactly how many enterprises responded to tax rate changes.

A dominant theme of this analysis of responsibility is to emphasize constraints, pressures, and social requisites, avoiding the complexities of motivation. It is behavior, not intent, that counts in the final analysis. Social responsibility refers to actions and choices for whatever reason, with the ambiguities of motivation better left to mind readers or analytical psychiatrists.

Another controversial error is to extrapolate social responsibility into a halfway house on the road to socialism. Executives conceived of as acting beyond check and balance governmental powers as responsible managers in a free society would only have those capacities temporarily. They would be transferred to a constitutional bureaucracy. Recent work with social responsibility, however, suggests that it relates to a market system functioning in an evolving sociocultural environment that constrains and directs business behavior.

A fear of socialism as a near cousin to social responsibility arises from an overly simplified application of the standard economics paradigm, which visualizes market economies devoid of interchange with a sociocultural system. A more accurate understanding of the modern world is in terms of the organization theory and institutional, social economics' conceptual maps of current reality.

NOTES

1. A reasonably thorough discussion of socioeconomic performance criteria for the American economy is found in Harold L. Johnson, *Business in Contemporary Society: Framework and Issues* (Belmont, Calif.: Wadsworth, 1971), pp. 1-20.

2. See Talcott Parsons and Neil J. Smelser, *Economy and Society: A Study in the Integration of Economic and Social Theory* (New York: Free Press, 1956).

3. See Raymond Bauer, "The Future of Corporate Social Accounting," in Meinholf Dierkes and Raymond Bauer, *Corporate Social Accounting* (New York: Praeger, 1973).

4. Edward S. Mason, ed. *The Large Corporation in Modern Society* (Cambridge, Mass.: Harvard University Press, 1960), p. 205.

5. See R. A. Schwartz, "Corporate Philanthropic Contributions," *Journal of Finance*, June, 1968, pp. 479-97.

To complicate matters, however, the Schwartz study indicates that corporate donations were more responsive to cash-flow changes than to those of income, as were advertising expenditures. Hence, assuming advertising outlays are profit-oriented, then the similar response with contributions suggests that they may be profit-oriented as well.[5]

3

STUDIES AND SURVEYS
SET THE PARAMETERS

The review thus far has demonstrated the general nature and basis of social responsibility, setting the stage for presentation of its details and, in turn, of the content of corporate social reporting. In a sociocultural system there are two possible sources of information about the system's goals, norms, and values, about the general variables and parameters or details of the systemic requisites. Professional investigators, the "experts," so to speak, who have probed the dimensions of social performance of business, can give their judgments. Their analyses and studies can give significant clues. Perhaps more satisfying, however, is to hear from members of society, who because they operate in the system know a great deal about performance criteria and social expectations. Thus, it is useful to see what practicing executives and other participants have concluded social responsibility involves and what the components of corporate social disclosure are. What are U.S. corporations actually doing about CSR? It is readily apparent from these sources of information that considerable precision has been established about what these interrelated topics include.

Looking first to the experts, in 1972-73 the National Association of Accountants (NAA) established a Committee on Accounting for Corporate Social Performance consisting of eight members. This group of presumably knowledgeable observers wrestled with the issues of social responsibility, issuing their first report in 1974.[1] Their checklist of major areas of social performance is contained in Table 3.1. This detailed listing classified under the general headings of community involvement, human resources, physical resources, environmental contributions, and product or service contributions is largely self-explanatory. It is sufficient to note that this taxonomy of social responsibility developed by a group of

TABLE 3.1

Major Areas of Social Performance as Outlined by the National Association of Accountants Committee on Accounting for Corporate Social Performance, 1974

Community involvement

1. General philanthropy—corporate support of educational institutions, cultural activities, recreational programs, health and community welfare agencies, and similar eleemosynary organizations
2. Public and private transportation—alleviating or preventing urban transportation problems, including the provision of mass transportation of employees
3. Health services—providing health care facilities and services and the support of programs to reduce disease and illness
4. Housing—improving the standard of dwellings, the construction of needed dwellings, and the financing of housing renovation and construction
5. Aid in personal and business problems—alleviation of problems related to the physically handicapped, child care, minority businesses, disadvantaged persons, and the like
6. Community planning and improvement—programs of urban planning and renewal, crime prevention, and the like
7. Volunteer activities—encouraging and providing time for employees to be active as volunteers in community activities
8. Specialized food programs—the provision of meals to meet the dietary needs of the aged, the infirm, the disadvantaged child, and other groups
9. Education—the development and implementation of educational programs to supplement those of the public or private schools, such as work study programs, and employee service on school boards, school authorities, and college university trustee and advisory boards

Human resources

1. Employment practices—providing equal job opportunities for all persons, creation of summer job opportunities for students, and recruiting in depressed areas
2. Training programs—providing programs for all employees to increase their skills, earning potential, and job satisfaction
3. Promotion policies—recognizing the abilities of all employees and providing equal opportunities for promotion
4. Employment continuity—scheduling production so as to minimize layoffs and recalls, maintaining facilities in efficient operating condition so that they will not have to be abandoned because of deterioration, and exploring all feasible alternatives to closing a facility
5. Remuneration—maintaining a level of total salaries and wages plus benefits that is in line with others in either the industry or community
6. Working conditions—providing safe, healthful, and pleasant working environment
7. Drugs and alcohol—providing education and counseling for employees to prevent or alleviate problems in these and similar areas
8. Job enrichment—providing the most meaningful work experiences practical for all employees
9. Communications—establishing and maintaining two-way communication between all levels of employees to secure suggestions, to provide information as to what the company is actu-

ally doing and how each department's activities relate to the total corporate activity, and to inform employees' families and friends of corporate activities

Physical resources and environmental contributions

1. Air—timely meeting of the law and going beyond the law in avoiding the creation of, alleviating, or eliminating pollutants in these areas
2. Water—timely meeting of the law and going beyond the law in avoiding the creation of, alleviating, or eliminating pollutants in these areas
3. Sound—timely meeting of the law and going beyond the law in avoiding the creation of, alleviating, or eliminating pollutants in these areas
4. Solid waste—disposal of solid waste in such a manner as to minimize contamination, reduce its bulk, and the like, and the design of processes and products that will minimize the creation of solid waste
5. Use of scarce resources—the conservation of existing energy sources, the development of new energy sources, and the conservation of scarce materials
6. Aesthetics—the design and location of facilities in conformance with surroundings and with pleasing architecture and landscaping

Product or service contributions

1. Completeness and clarity of labeling, packaging, and marketing representation—assurance that labeling and representation as to methods of use, limitations on use, hazards of use, shelf life, quantity of contents, and quality cannot be misunderstood
2. Warranty provisions—adherence to all stated or implied warranties of a product with implementation through timely recalls, repairs, or replacements
3. Responsiveness to consumer complaints—prompt and complete responses to all complaints received
4. Consumer education—literature and media programs to keep consumers informed of product or service characteristics, methods and areas of use of products, and of planned product changes or discontinuances
5. Product quality—assurance through adequate control, "quality assurance," that quality is at least equal to what customers may reasonably expect on the basis of company representations
6. Product safety—design or formulation and packaging of products to minimize possibilities of harm or injury in product use
7. Content and frequency of advertising—giving full consideration to the omission of any media material that may be adverse or offensive and the avoidance of repetition to the extent that it becomes repugnant
8. Constructive research—orienting technical and market research to meet defined social needs and to avoid creating social and environmental problems or to minimize such problems; that is, energy consumption

Source: Wayne Keller, Chairman, Committee on Accounting for Social Performance, "Accounting for Corporate Social Performance," *Management Accounting*, February 1974, p. 41. Reprinted by permission.

accountant researchers is characterized for the most part by considerable detail and precision.

Another example of an effort to delineate the content of social responsibility and to measure business performance is seen in the research of Steven C. Dilley and Jerry C. Weygandt, two accountant scholars. In their development of a social responsibility annual report (SRAR), tested with data of an electric power company, they have structured several subreports.[2] These reports address the occupational health and safety record, minority and female recruitment and promotion patterns, environmental and pollution consequences of production activities, and community relations efforts, such as charitable contributions and facility beautification. Tables 3.2 and 3.3 illustrate the format of their effort at accounting for social responsibility. The significant aspects of their research for this discussion are the categories of their SRAR and their relative success in presenting data on these areas.

As a provocative illustration of efforts by informed students to categorize various elements of social responsibility, the information of Table 3.4 is presented. This material summarizes possible elements of responsibility as developed by a group of accountant-scholars at Texas A & M University.[3] Results of a survey of approximately 700 financial executives about this classification are also depicted. The categories are familiar, but the survey indicates a diversity of judgment, surprising in some instances and unexpected in others. The area of environmental control appears to be one of general consensus among these respondents, while the employment of women and minorities, at least as an area for disclosure of information, has a low rate of acceptance. Perhaps fear of confrontation or threat of court suits prompted many financial executives to conclude such data should not be published. It is important, however, to emphasize due to the strong constituency base of social responsibility and CSR, financial executives most likely cannot freely exercise their own preference. Female and minority employees and executives could be expected to place heavy weight on reporting about the employment and promotion status of their cohorts.

In another survey of important observer-participants in the contemporary business system, 261 accounting leaders were asked to evaluate whether the four NAA-defined areas of corporate social performance were important enough to be included in an information system.[4] As Table 3.5 depicts, there is considerable agreement that a reporting procedure for these categories should be provided, implying that these are indeed elements of social responsibility. This finding varies somewhat from the Strawser study, for reporting on human resources is strongly supported in this survey, with over 96 percent agreeing that information should be made available for this category. It may be that such strong support for these four elements reflects their "God, Mother, Country, and Apple Pie" nature; it is difficult to be critical of these performance areas. Such universal acceptance would characterize goals and norms held in a strong consensus by the American people.

TABLE 3.2

Dilley-Weygandt Social Responsibility, Annual Report, Part 1, 1973

Utility Company
Occupational Health and Safety Statement for the Period July 1, 1971 to December 31, 1971*

Average number of employees during the period	500
Total hours worked by all employees	403,000
On-the-job fatalities during the period	None
Number of workdays lost due to on-the-job injuries	35
Number of employees affected	6
Percent of total employees	1.2
Number of workdays lost due to occupational illness	0
Number of employees affected	0
Percent of total employees	0

Utility Company
Minorities Recruitment and Promotion Statement, 1971

Total population of community	300,000
Percent minorities	1.1
Total number of employees	500
Total number of minority black and Spanish-surnamed employees	9
Subject to union contracts	8
Percent of all employees subject to union contracts	2.2
Percent of all employees	1.6
Supervisory and professional staff	1
Percent of all supervisory and professional staff	0.7
Percent of all employees	0.2
Total number of female employees	83
Subject to union contracts	71
Percent of all employees subject to union contracts	19.9
Percent of all employees	14.2
Supervisory and professional staff	12
Percent of all supervisory and professional staff	8.6
Percent of all employees	2.4
Special minority recruitment and advancement programs	
Black and Spanish-surnamed employees	None
Dollars spent	0
Females	None
Dollars spent	0

*The data for this statement were derived from OSHA Form 1033. The information contained on that report is required by the Williams-Steiger Occupational Health and Safety Act. The initial reporting period ran from July 1, 1971 to December 31, 1971. Subsequent reporting periods will run from January 1 to December 31 of each year.

Source: Steven C. Dilley and Jerry J. Weygandt, "Measuring Social Responsibility: An Empirical Test," *Journal of Accountancy*, September 1973, p. 68. Copyright© 1973 by the American Institute of Certified Public Accountants, Inc. Reprinted by permission.

TABLE 3.3

Dilley-Weygandt Social Responsibility, Annual Report, Part 2, 1973
(in dollars)

Utility Company
Statement of Funds Flow for Socially Relevant Activities, 1971

Environmental	
Installation of electrostatic precipitators[a]	26,000
Construction of power plants[b]	2,089,000
Construction of transmission lines[c]	35,000
Electrical substation beautification[d]	142,000
Incremental cost of low-sulfur coal[e]	33,670
Conversion of service vehicles to use of propane gas[f]	3,700
Incremental cost of underground electric installations[g]	737,000
Incremental cost of silent jackhammers[h]	100
Environmental research	
Thermal	17,500
Nuclear	1,955
Other	38,575
Subtotal	57,530
Total	3,124,000
Other benefits	
Charitable contributions	26,940
Employee educational and recreational expenditures[i]	6,000

22

Total other benefits	32,940
Total 1971 funds flow for socially relevant activities	3,156,940
As a percentage of 1971 operating revenues	7.9
As a percentage of 1971 advertising expenses	8,500

[a]The company will complete installation of two electrostatic precipitators in 1973. Costs in 1971 totaled $26,000.

[b]The company is building power plants that will begin operation in the middle to late 1970s. Incremental cash costs of environmental controls installed in these plants during 1971 totaled $2,089,000.

[c]The company is constructing a high-voltage transmission line from another community to the company's service area. Environmental cash costs resulting from wider spacing of line towers totaled $35,000 in 1971.

[d]The company constructed a new substation in 1971 with an enclosed structure rather than open exposure of the electric transformers. The cost of this enclosure along with landscaping of existing substations totaled $142,000 in 1971.

[e]The company used approximately 150,000 tons of coal during 1971 for electric power generation. Low-sulfur content coal comprised 8.6 percent of this coal consumption with the remaining 91.4 percent being coal of a higher sulfur content. The low-sulfur coal cost approximately $2.61 per ton more than the high-sulfur coal.

[f]Motor vehicles fueled with propane gas contribute substantially less air pollutants to the atmosphere than gasoline-fueled vehicles. During 1971 the company converted 9 more of its fleet of 115 vehicles to use of propane gas. The cost of this conversion was $3,700. Seventeen company vehicles are now operated on propane gas.

[g]Underground installation of electric transmission lines has increased since environmental attention has focused on the aesthetic pollution of poles and wires. During 1971 the company installed underground electric transmission lines, which cost $737,000 more than putting the same lines above ground.

[h]Jackhammers used by the company are, with one exception, of the normal, noise-polluting type. One jackhammer purchased during 1971 with noise controls cost $100 more than the regular jackhammers.

[i]The company reimburses employees for educational expenditures and provides recreational opportunities such as the annual company picnic. Such expenditures amounted to approximately $6,000 in 1971.

Source: Steven C. Dilley and Jerry J. Weygandt, "Measuring Social Responsibility: An Empirical Test," *Journal of Accountancy,* September 1973, p. 69. Copyright ©1973 by the American Institute of Certified Public Accountants, Inc. Reprinted by permission.

TABLE 3.4

The Content of Social Reports according to "The Financial Community," 1974-75

Possible Categories of Information	Percentage of Agreement*		
	Controllers	CPAs	CFAs
Environmental controls			
Prevention or abatement of pollution	74	70	79
Reducing pollutive effects of products	71	68	73
Recycling of waste materials	54	62	64
Repair of environment	68	68	82
Product improvement in the public interest			
Safety improvements	71	66	80
Quality improvements	68	68	82
Community activities (mixed interest)			
Donations of cash or services	51	52	54
Sponsoring public health projects	39	52	39
Aid to education and the arts	38	51	38
Responsibility to personnel (mixed interest)			
Personnel counseling	19	40	37
Assisting displaced employees	29	53	39
Employee training and education	40	60	59
Employment of women and minorities (lean interest)			
Employment of women	32	26	39
Employment of racial minorities	40	34	39
Advancement of racial minorities or women	34	33	38

* All other respondents were either neutral or did not agree that the information listed should be reported.

Source: Robert H. Strawser, Keith G. Stanga, and James J. Benjamin, "Social Reporting: Financial Community Views," *CPA Journal*, February 1976, p. 7. Reprinted by permission.

TABLE 3.5

Accounting Leaders' Evaluation of Proposed Corporate Social Performance Areas, 1974
(261 respondents)

Performance areas	Strongly Agree	Agree	Indifferent	Disagree	Strongly Disagree
	Percentage Distribution of Responses				
12. A social performance information system should provide a basis for reporting on the following major areas of social performance:	—	—	—	—	—
A. Community involvement—activities that primarily benefit the general public, such as philanthropy, provision of health care, and the like	16.6	75.1	7.8	0.5	0.0
B. Human resources—activities directed toward the well-being of employees, such as training programs, employment practices, promotion policies, working conditions, and the like	32.3	64.0	2.3	0.9	0.5
C. Physical resources and environmental contributions—activities directed toward alleviating or preventing environmental deterioration, such as control of air, water, and noise pollution, and the like	29.0	65.9	5.1	0.0	0.0
D. Product or service contributions—customer relations and effects of products or services on society, such as labeling and packaging requirements, advertising practices, product quality and safety, and the like	22.8	66.5	9.8	0.9	0.0

Source: A. H. Barnett, "Accounting for Corporate Social Performance: A Survey," *Management Accounting*, November 1974, p. 25. Reprinted by permission.

Having obtained the judgments of knowledgeable observers, what clues are to be found in a study of executives and of corporate behavior itself? Data from several surveys indicate some tentative findings about the parameters or particulars of responsibility. In a survey of 96 large U.S. corporations, some significant patterns are apparent, as indicated in the data of Table 3.6.[5] Some categories of activity are widely practiced, while others are less important. Areas of minority hiring and training, the environment, and contributions to education rank high; virtually none of the respondents from large corporations ranked contributions to the arts, truth in advertising, or understandable accounting statements as high priority items in social responsibility. This research also indicates that larger firms generally engage in more social responsibility activity than do smaller establishments, perhaps because of their greater visibility in a media-saturated world.

Another noteworthy survey of 284 leading U.S. corporations was conducted under the sponsorship of the Committee for Economic Development (CED), the principal investigators being John J. Corson and George A. Steiner, and was published in 1974.[6] The data presented in Table 3.7 about the activities of these corporations is most revealing, for here is at least a prima facie definition of the content of social responsibility. What companies are actually doing with varied social and economic programs can be taken as an operational statement of responsibility. As the rankings indicate, minority employment, training, advancement, and educational grants are prime elements on the responsibility agenda, followed by pollution abatement and attention directed to productivity improvements. With minority employment and promotion a strong component of responsibility, the conclusions of financial community representatives that reporting on this area is unimportant, as noted in the Strawser study, is all the more incongruous. It would seem apparent that the most important aspects of social responsibility as revealed by behavior would necessitate a concomitant reporting on goals and results.

Another manifestation of the operational meaning of responsibility and of the priorities within it can be seen from a study of annual reports of 47 selected corporations, the firms listed in Table 3.8. The most frequently mentioned areas of reporting included environmental quality (primarily water pollution); equal employment opportunities; product safety; educational aid; charitable donations; industrial safety; employee benefits; and community support programs.[7] The information in Table 3.8 offers some significant clues about the priorities within that set, for it is apparent from the reporting distribution that environment, the catchall category of education/charities and health, and minority opportunities are much more widely reported than are consumerism and safety, for example.

The supposition is that activities described in annual reports are a close indicator of the actual range of behavior, a reasonable proposition. One characteristic of social responsibility, however, is that over time it is quite likely to see some shifting priorities. Areas of activity such as minority and female employment are unlikely to diminish sharply in importance, but some items such as con-

TABLE 3.6

Types of Social Responsibility Activity Believed Most Important among Large U.S. Corporations, 1973
(96 firms)

Activity	Number Practicing	Firms Ranking Activity among Top Three	
		Number	Percent
Minority hiring	75	40	53
Ecology	75	35	47
Minority training	65	23	35
Contributions to education	82	23	28
Consumer complaints	44	9	20
Urban renewal	51	8	16
Civil rights	51	8	16
Product defects	34	3	9
Contributions to the arts	65	5	8
Hard-core training	53	4	8
Truth in advertising	40	3	8
Hard-core hiring	56	2	4
Consumer-oriented label changes	23	1	4
Guarantees and warranties	31	1	3
Understandable accounting statements	40	0	0

Source: Henry Eilbirt and I. Robert Parket, "The Current Status of Social Responsibility," *Business Horizons*, August 1973, p. 10. Copyright ©1973 by the Foundation of the School of Business at Indiana University. Reprinted by permission.

sumerism and product safety at the time of the survey in 1974 may have been rising to the attention of executives.[8] The task of the manager administering limited resources is a formidable one with such a crowding of the social responsibility agenda, as few requirements sink into oblivion with the advent of new obligations.

As an alternative hypothesis, consumerism and employee or product safety may have been regarded as categories of normal business activity and hence not to be mentioned in some kind of social reporting. A shifting force of emphasis upon categories of responsibility gives corporations an opportunity to "lead the pack" in innovating policies in developing areas of responsibility. Whirlpool Cor-

TABLE 3.7

Social and Economic Programs of Large U.S. Corporations, 1974
(284 firms)

Activity	Number of Companies Indicating Involvement	Ten Most Frequent Activities
Economic growth and efficiency		
Increasing productivity in the private sector of the economy	180	6
Improving the innovativeness and performance of business management	174	
Enhancing competition	69	
Cooperating with the government in developing more effective measures to control inflation and achieve high levels of employment	121	
Supporting fiscal and monetary policies for steady economic growth	109	
Helping with the post-Vietnam conversion of the economy	37	
Education		
Direct financial aid to schools, including scholarships, grants, and tuition refunds	238	2
Support for increases in school budgets	38	
Donation of equipment and skilled personnel	139	
Assistance in curriculum development	83	
Aid in counseling and remedial education	67	
Establishment of new schools, running schools, and school systems	38	
Assistance in the management and financing of colleges	120	
Employment and training		
Active recruitment of the disadvantaged	199	3
Special functional training, remedial education, and counseling	134	
Provision of day care centers for children of working mothers	26	
Improvement of work/career opportunities	191	4
Retraining of workers affected by automation or other causes of joblessness	80	
Establishment of company programs to remove the hazards of old age and sickness	139	
Supporting where needed and appropriate the extension of government accident, unemployment, health, and retirement systems	93	
Civil rights and equal opportunity		
Ensuring employment and advancement opportunities for minorities	244	1
Facilitating equality of results by continued training and other special programs	176	

Activity	Number of Companies Indicating Involvement	Ten Most Frequent Activities
Supporting and aiding the improvement of black educational facilities, and special programs for blacks and other minorities in integrated institutions	159	
Encouraging adoption of open-housing ordinances	31	
Building plants and sales offices in the ghettos	39	
Providing financing and managerial assistance to minority enterprises, and participating with minorities in joint ventures	134	
Urban renewal and development		
Leadership and financial support for city and regional planning and development	135	
Building or improving low-income housing	75	
Building shopping centers, new communities, new cities	78	
Improving transportation systems	88	
Pollution abatement		
Installation of modern equipment	189	5
Engineering new facilities for minimum environmental effects	169	10
Research and technological development	145	
Cooperating with municipalities in joint treatment facilities	84	
Cooperating with local, state, regional, and federal agencies in developing improved systems of environmental management	126	
Developing more effective programs for recycling and reusing disposable materials	97	
Conservation and recreation		
Augmenting the supply of replenishable resources, such as trees, with more productive species	42	
Preserving animal life and the ecology of forests and comparable areas	41	
Providing recreational and aesthetic facilities for public use	80	
Restoring aesthetically depleted properties such as strip mines	38	
Improving the yield of scarce materials and recycling to conserve the supply	61	

(continued)

TABLE 3.7 *(continued)*

Activity	*Number of Companies Indicating Involvement*	*Ten Most Frequent Activities*
Culture and the arts		
Direct financial support to art institutions and the performing arts	177	7
Development of indirect support as a business expense through gifts in kind, sponsoring artistic talent, and advertising	96	
Participation on boards to give advice on legal, labor, and financial management problems	138	
Helping secure government financial support for local or state arts councils and the National Endowment for the Arts	49	
Medical care		
Helping plan community health activities	111	
Designing and operating low-cost medical-care programs	42	
Designing and running new hospitals, clinics, and extended-care facilities	42	
Improving the administration and effectiveness of medical care	89	
Developing better systems for medical education, nurses' training	52	
Developing and supporting a better national system of health care	40	
Government		
Helping improve management performance at all levels of government	100	
Supporting adequate compensation and development programs for government executives and employees	31	
Working for the modernization of the nation's governmental structure	51	
Facilitating the reorganization of government to improve its responsiveness and performance	69	
Advocating and supporting reforms in the election system and the legislative process	39	
Designing programs to enhance the effectiveness of the civil services	22	
Promoting reforms in the public welfare system, law enforcement, and other major governmental operations	62	

Source: John C. Corson and George A. Steiner, *Measuring Business's Social Performance: The Corporate Social Audit* (New York: Committee for Economic Development, 1974), pp. 27-29. Reprinted by permission.

TABLE 3.8

Corporate Social Reporting of 47 Selected Corporations, 1975

Corporations That Report Some Aspect of Social Responsibility	Environment	Consumerism	Education/Charities/Health	Community Participation	Minority Opportunities	Safety
Abbott Laboratories			x	x		
Abt Associates						
Allied Chemical	x		x			
American Bakeries			x	x		
American Smelting and Refining	x					
Bank of America	x	x	x	x	x	
R. G. Barry						
Carnation Co.	x		x		x	
Carrier Corp.			x			
Chrysler Corp.	x	x	x		x	
Cummins Engine				x		
Doyle Dane Bernbach				x		
E. I. duPont	x		x	x	x	x
Eastern Gas and Fuel Associates			x		x	x
Eli Lilly and Co.			x			
First National Bank of Minneapolis						
First Pennsylvania Bank					x	
General Electric	x		x			
General Foods		x	x		x	
General Mills			x	x		
General Motors			x	x		
Hercules Inc.	x					
Hudson Pulp and Paper			x			

(continued)

TABLE 3.8 (*continued*)

Corporations That Report Some Aspect of Social Responsibility	Environment	Consumerism	Education/Charities/Health	Community Participation	Minority Opportunities	Safety
Inland Steel Co.	x		x			
International Paper	x		x		x	
I.T.T.	x		x	x	x	
Louisville Cement	x					
Marcor	x	x			x	
Monsanto	x	x				
Oscar Mayer and Company	x		x	x	x	
Owens-Corning Fiberglas	x		x	x	x	
Owens-Illinois	x				x	x
Pfizer	x		x		x	
Phillips Screw	x					
Polaroid				x	x	
P.P.G. Industries Inc.	x				x	
Quaker Oats Company			x		x	
Reynolds Metals	x				x	x
Rohm and Hass					x	
Scovill Manufacturing	x	x	x	x	x	
Standard Oil (Indiana)	x			x	x	
Union Camp Corp.			x			
Union Carbide Corp.			x	x	x	x
U.S. Steel	x		x			
Walter Kidd and Co.			x			
Westvaco Corp.	x					
Xerox			x			

Source: Nabil Elias and Marc Epstein, "Dimensions of Corporate Social Reporting," *Management Accounting*, March 1975, p. 38. Reprinted by permission.

TABLE 3.9

Social Responsibility Disclosure by the Fortune 500 Corporations, 1971-76

	1976	*1974*	*1973*	*1972*	*1971*
Companies making social responsibility disclosures	425	346	298	286	239
Companies with no social responsibility disclosures	75	151	198	206	226
Reports not readily available	0	3	4	8	35
Total	500	500	500	500	500
Percentage making social responsibility disclosure	75	69.2	59.6	57.2	47.8

Source: Dennis R. Beresford, "Social Responsibility Disclosure Grows," *Management Accounting*, May 1977, p. 56; and Dennis R. Bereford and Stewart A. Feldman, "Companies Increase Social Responsibility Disclosures," *Management Accounting*, March 1976, p. 51. Reprinted by permission.

poration, for example, very probably has experienced a payoff of increased repeat sales and public relations benefits from pioneer consumer relations programs.

All of the studies reported thus far have been surveys of particular populations, samples that have the perplexing pattern of partial returns and self-selection biasing results. The most likely expectation is that responding individuals and corporations are those most sensitive and proactive to responsibility requirements. The content of social responsibility is probably not affected by the phenomena of self-selection, but it may overstate the extent to which firms are actively meeting the signals of social expectations.

An Ernst and Ernst survey, conducted over several years by Dennis R. Beresford, however, is a *census* of the *Fortune* 500 companies that examines the extent and character of social responsibility disclosure.[9] The categories chosen by this experienced observer include the familiar ones of environment, equal opportunity, personnel, community involvement, products, and other activities such as corporate reorganization as related to responsibility and development of codes of ethics. Each of his general groupings has considerable specificity. For example, under personnel-selected items are promotion of employee health and safety, disclosure of accident statistics, training, and counseling in alcoholism or drug-related problems.

The obvious conclusion to be drawn from his annual surveys of social responsibility disclosure is that more companies are doing it. A virtual bandwagon of reporting on these topics has been rolling for large U.S. corporations since 1971, as the data of Table 3.9 reflects. Obviously, most of these presentations could be counted on to be self-serving to some degree, glorifying the role of the firm in these areas, indicating the benefits of company policies with little information about the adverse impact of production or policy upon corporate constituents.

Nonetheless, the fact that most large corporations have seen fit to make reports even with these disabilities is revealing support for the proposition that company executives know what they are supposed to report about and feel social pressures to do so. The content of responsibility is not some vague do-goodism but relates to particular socioeconomic goals and norms of business practice. All of the surveys, even those limited by self-selection, indicate that participants in the business system know what the operational definitions of social responsibility are and to what categories CSR relates.

At this stage of discussion, debate, and policy no one can pretend not to know the variables and particular parameters of corporate social responsibility. If imprecision or obscurity of meaning are proposed, it means either someone has not done their homework or that they are engaged in an exercise of obfuscation aimed at confusion instead of clarification. The investigations briefly summarized here, only part of a considerable literature, indicate considerable detail about the range and specificity of responsibility.

NOTES

1. Wayne Keller, Chairman, The Committee on Accounting for Social Performance, "Accounting for Corporate Social Performance," *Management Accounting*, February 1974, p. 41.

2. Steven C. Dilley and Jerry J. Weygandt, "Measuring Social Responsibility: An Empirical Test," *Journal of Accounting*, September 1973, pp. 62-70.

3. Robert H. Strawser, Keith G. Stranga, and James J. Benjamin, "Social Reporting: Financial Community Views," *CPA Journal*, February 1976, p. 7.

4. A. H. Barnett, "Accounting for Corporate Social Performance: A Survey," *Management Accounting*, November 1974, p. 25.

5. Henry Eibirt and I. Robert Parket, "The Current Status of Corporate Social Responsibility," *Business Horizons*, August 1973, pp. 9-10.

6. John J. Corson and George A. Steiner, *Measuring Business's Social Performance: The Corporate Social Audit* (New York: Committee for Economic Development, 1974).

7. Nabil Elias and Marc Epstein, "Dimensions of Corporate Social Reporting, *Management Accounting*, March 1975, p. 38.

8. "Corporate Clout for Consumers," *Business Week*, September 12, 1977, pp. 144-45.

9. Dennis R. Beresford, "Social Responsibility Disclosure Grows," *Management Accounting*, May 1977, pp. 56-60; and Dennis R. Beresford and Stewart A. Feldman, "Companies Increase Social Responsibility Disclosure," *Management Accounting*, March 1976, pp. 51-55.

4

THE RATIONALE FOR CSR

As we have seen, social responsibility and CSR have moved beyond mere rhetoric and ideological battles to a strong conceptual base and increased specificity. But pragmatic Americans, and undoutedly others as well, are generally not overly impressed with the topic as it is discussed. What is the value or use of CSR? What are the benefits and costs that can be expected to flow from its use, making it a worthwhile venture for American business? These are the questions usually posed at this point.

A satisfactory way to answer these questions is by appealing to a multifaceted rationale, first introducing arguments connected to the preceding discussion and then moving the analysis in two directions, initially to a broad, macro, systemic case for CSR and finally to a micro, managerial, organizationally oriented set of proposals. The preceding discussion has attempted to establish that U.S. business's standards for performance evaluation encompass more than expanding output and profits, though these may indeed be important criteria. It also developed an image of accountability and stewardship broader than simply that of shareholders in large corporations. The implicit "social contract" between business and society includes terms and conditions relating to a number of constituencies or organizational participants.

Table 4.1 lists the considerable number of groups interested in CSR, both interest groups or "publics" more closely associated with corporate life as well as various governmental agencies, activist groups, and professional bodies. In brief, the case for CSR is that it facilitates evaluation of corporate behavior by these varied participants given diverse social and economic performance criteria. A communication of information dealing with possible gaps between corporate behavior and standards seems essential in the discharge of accountability and managerial stewardship. It is perhaps simply the American mentality at work, where the scorekeeping question of "how are we doing" is commonplace. Yet, reasonable evaluation, the inescapable task of rational individuals, requires data on goals and results.

Information for assessing progress toward social performance requirements can be at a national, or macro, level, as is a great deal of the data presently available. Information about unemployment, levels of GNP, occupational fatality and injury statistics, and citizen consumer surveys of attitudes about U.S. business are currently being collected and published. Reporting on social performance at the firm level—by definition a microlevel set of socioeconomic data—may complement aggregate data clusters.

Participants in individual corporations, as well as the general community, find micro data on corporations important for personal decision making. Does the safety record of firm A in comparison with firm B suggest that employee exodus or agitation are warranted? How does industry X's record in employment or supplier discrimination compare with industry Y's? Individual employees, unions, and civil rights organizations would find such information most valuable. This kind of microsocial data can be expected to facilitate rational decision making in evaluating corporate performance and the consequent choices by individuals and groups associated with particular firms or industries.

Traditional economics' picture of the association of employees, suppliers, or dealers with the firm, for example, is that they freely exchange their services or productive inputs for a compensation package that includes both cash and nonmonetary elements. No one pretends that individuals work solely for income, profits, or wealth. Looking at the employment nexus, prestige, safety, security, and personal integrity are among the nonmonetary elements sought from a job along with cash.

It is relatively easy to evaluate the cash consequences of an employment transaction, but the nonmonetary dimensions often are obscured by a fog of uncertainty and ignorance. CSR offers information on the noncash dimensions of market transactions, thereby facilitating a monitoring of the total benefit/cost configuration of association with a corporation. Risk of accident, health hazard, layoffs, or of arbitrary cessation of contractual arrangements, as with suppliers and dealers, are some of the social data relevant to individual decision making.

Picking up the stick of corporate responsibility from the other end, that is, that of managerial accountability, it would appear obvious that responsibility cannot be exercised unless it is clear what expectations are and how behavior coincides with social requisites. It is thus a dual evaluation—by the general citizenry and coalition members making up the corporate organization *and* by managers who as prime decision makers coordinate corporate affairs. Evaluation without data and description of social performance is judgment left in a thoroughly subjective limbo.

TABLE 4.1

Potential Users of Corporate Social Performance Information

Internal

| Directors | Other employees | Public relations department |
| Management | Union local | Law department |

External

Associated

Investors and lenders—especially churches, foundations, banks, insurance companies, universities, and mutual funds
Customers
Suppliers

Government

Securities and Exchange Commission
Environmental Protection Agency
Equal Employment Opportunity Commission
Department of Housing and Urban Development
Internal Revenue Service
General Accounting Office
Congress, state legislatures, city commissions
Law enforcement agencies
Regulatory agencies and commissions at all levels (FTC, FCC, ICC, and the like)

Public interest groups

Project on Corporate Responsibility	Council for Corporate Review
Council on Economic Priorities	Citizens Action Program
Accountants for the Public Interest	Tax Action Group
Corporate Accountability Research Group	Common Cause
Agribusiness Accountability Project	Public Citizen, Inc.
Investor Responsibility Research Center	NAACP
American Civil Liberties Union	Public Communication, Inc.
San Francisco Consumer Action	Sierra Club
National Affiliation of Concerned Business	Wilderness Society
Students	Friends of the Earth

Other

News media	Financial Analysts Federation
Stock exchanges	Researchers
American Institute of Certified Public	Educators
Accountants	Students and other potential employees
American Accounting Association	General public
National Association of Accountants	

Source: Ralph Estes, *Corporate Social Accounting* (New York: Wiley Interscience, 1976), p. 4. Reprinted by permission.

A related extension to this aspect of the case for CSR flows from the accountant's concept of *contingent liability*. An enterprise undoubtedly can increase short-term profits by skimping on resource allocations toward fulfilling social expectations. Nearby public water resources can be polluted, a dangerous work environment encouraged, layoffs or plant closures carried out, more in the manner of a century ago rather than according to the norms of today, as means of cutting costs or boosting short-term revenues. Given the current climate of opinion, however, these birds of expediency can be expected to return home to roost in some future accounting period, with disastrous repercussions for the organization. Poor morale and consequent lower productivity, accelerating pollution control costs, fewer repeat sales, and expanded government regulation are the likely future consequences of present antisocial behavior.

In analogous ways some railroads in earlier decades, perhaps out of a perceived business necessity, improved the short-term look of their books by postponing necessary maintenance of roadbeds and equipment, although this placed their operations in severe financial jeopardy. Delayed maintenance and poor current social performance both introduce contingent liabilities of which investors and creditors should be informed. Poor social performance in all probability pays off in trouble later—so data on such contingent difficulties is valuable information for present and potential investors as well as creditor participants in a corporation.

Moving now to a more macro element in the rationale for CSR, the whole area of social responsibility and the associated process of CSR can be addressed in another language, that of standard economics. In the vocabulary of conventional microeconomics, much of these materials are instances of negative or positive externalities, side effects of production that are not fully captured in market transactions. The classic illustration of negative side effects is that of water pollution, where persons not compensated nonetheless bear real costs of the output of commodities. The term "side effects" may imply relatively minor adverse or positive impacts on individuals not linked in the exchange process. But as in the instance of some drugs, externalities may on occasion crucially influence the well-being of large portions of the population.

Economics at an elementary level may tend to focus only on a limited range of consequences of the input/output process, those in the contractual link between buyer and seller, but welfare investigations have an extensive history of exploring externality phenomena. Thus, social responsibility of business can be translated into reducing the social injuries or negative side effects of business affairs, hardly a novel idea. In this framework CSR is the presentation of microsocial indicators that quantify or describe the extent and incidence of extramarket side effects.

One consequence of negative and positive externalities of business activity is the misallocation of resources, for with adverse side effects linked with production the full costs of that production are not borne by the market. A consequent underpricing leads to an excess amount of output, while the opposite result is the case with social benefits from production not charged for by the corporation. These misallocations of resources have been addressed for many years by economic analysts, and the proposals for at least a diminution of the inefficiencies of externalities include private negotiation, pollution taxes, and government regulation.

What is the best or optimal externality policy? A priori, armchair theorizing offers useful insights into the various advantages and disadvantages. But in the end the decision is made on the grubby ground of an empirical, detailed examination of the adverse side effects. It is facts that lead to answers. As descriptive indicators providing details by firm and industry on the extent of such micro side effects as water pollution or industrial health hazards, corporate social reporting can assist toward better solutions. In this world of second best, analysis in conjunction with microdata on side effects can lead to better solutions.

The next social, or macroargument for CSR comes from the perpetual, fundamental dilemma of social control. Individuals can be expected to pursue their own interests whatever their circumstances. Indeed, the opportunity and merit to "doing one's thing" has been a value emphasized in American culture. But this emphasis upon self-interest is held in tension with the goal that other individuals should not be disadvantaged in relationships where self-interest is the motivating force. Stated a little differently, society requires that the community interest be served along with self-interest and freedom.

Thus, a fundamental problem is how to reconcile these opposites into an energetic pursuit of self-interest without disadvantaging others. Individualistic interplay is to be one in which the community benefit is achieved. The difficulty is that all existing vehicles of social control by which self-interest and social welfare are reconciled, while obviously assisting in the reconciliation, nonetheless have serious deficiencies. None can be relied on altogether to solve the problem. The principal existing instruments of social control in economic affairs are the unconscious coordinators of behavior via the market and norms, role prescriptions, and social performance criteria and the formal, conscious direction of decision through law and governmental regulation.

This is not the place to spell out the strengths and weaknesses of each of these control institutions.[1] Suffice it to say that few individuals want to turn the task of social control over entirely to the tacit pressures of social norms and values, to the market, or to the requisites and compulsions of the government bureaucracy. In fact, at present, a general disillusionment and/or revulsion for control by government rule and law is widespread among the population. At the same time, though, few individuals desire to eliminate altogether the social coordination activities of either the market or government. Thoroughgoing market anarchists and socialist believers in total public control and planning are few in the United States.

There appears to be a sophisticated realization that simple panaceas will not lead to easy, utopian solutions to complex problems of social control. There is also a likelihood that corporate social reporting joined with relatively modest changes in corporate institution can help in diminishing the conflict between self-interest and social welfare. The ideas on which this proposition are based are partly familiar and partly novel. It is a commonplace dictum of police routine that crime can be reduced by increasing lighting and visibility. By analogy, disclosure is likely to have a similar impact on corporate behavior. Over 60 years ago, Supreme Court Justice Louis Brandeis suggested, "Publicity is justly commended as a remedy for social and industrial disease. Sunlight is said to be the best disinfectant; electric light the most efficient policeman."[2]

When business affairs take place in a goldfish bowl of publicity and information on social performance, considerable encouragement exists for behavior to conform to social norms and expectations. As some executives have proposed, you should not engage in any activity that you cannot reasonably defend before a national television audience.

The goldfish bowl/streetlight approach to social control relates not only to the external interface between the corporation and the community but also to the internal affairs of the enterprise. It is at this point that a note of novelty is introduced into the discussion. When a corporation's illegal or embarrassing activities have come to public attention, many top executives have argued they were totally ignorant of the whole affair. The chief executive of General Electric, for example, maintained that he was unaware of the extensive price conspiracies in the electrical equipment manufacturing industry of 20 years ago, conspiracies in which GE participated. This could conceivably come about by design, by underlings seeking to insulate "the boss" from dangerous information or it could be the typical consequence of bureaucratic inertia or politics.

A humorous example of an executive's ignorance of his own organization's behavior is captured in a *New Yorker* cartoon. Two men, perhaps Environmental Protection Agency officials, have taken a third person, presumably the factory's president, to the factory wall abutting a river. From there he can see pollution pouring through pipes into the river from the plant. With a comment of apparent surprise, he exclaims, "So *that's* where it goes! I'd like to thank you for bringing this to my attention."[3] Apparently it is not altogether an effort at homor to suggest that many top executives are unaware of the specific social impacts of corporate policies and actions.

This is the kind of blindness that can be expected from a total focus on narrow financial performance as summarized in annual income statements and balance sheets. It arises not from fundamental necessity or evil intent but from a trained incapacity to see the broader consequences of corporate behavior, an incapacity generated by excessive concentration on the corporation's profit performance.

Business executives like everyone else have been schooled to prefer clean water and air, safe factories, and a more open society; but without information concerning corporate impacts on these goals, executives cannot be expected to respond in the proper direction. Perception and awareness precede responsible behavior. To use the language of Christopher Stone, social control with less government intrusion requires that the *corporate information network be mended* and expanded to include data about the social performance of business.*

It is essential that the collected information be transmitted to company executives, directors, top officials, shareholders, and government so that the trained incapacity or blind spots of key decision makers be eliminated. Of course, a great deal of such reporting is already distributed to relevant government agencies. The novel argument here is that chief executives and other prime actors in the corporation *be required* to receive such information regularly. Under certain conditions this "mending" of the information network might require tailored social audits of company performance where a particular firm or industry has a record of deficiency in specific social expectations.

This modest institutional adjustment of the market system has the potential of bringing about a partial rollback of detailed government regulation. The light of publicity generated by CSR could be counted on to reinforce the influence of social norms and expectations, giving them teeth through increasing awareness both within and outside the organization. What this means is that CSR cannot be conceived of as a purely voluntary exercise on the part of large corporations. It must be a government-sanctioned disclosure of information on social performance.

This expansion of information disclosure to those both within and outside the corporation is hardly a radical institutional change. It is merely an adjustment of the constraints or rules of the game within which the enterprise system operates. It is far removed from a "socialistic intervention" into a "free enterprise" system. However, corporations and executives unwilling to operate in the glare of disclosures about social performance would find this aspect of the case for CSR less than fully convincing.

As a final macrolevel argument, CSR involves a two-way reporting between business and society. The public-at-large and interest groups, the custodians of particular social values, communicate what social expectations for American business are. Through law and norm they outline what the boundries and categories of CSR are to be. At the same time, business through its disclosures indicates something of corporate deeds with regard to these areas. Apart from this process of dialogue, and at the same time fundamental to it, however, society must make a benefit-cost type evaluation of its expectations of business. It is evident that healthy, safe work environments and a pollution-free atmosphere, while offering significant benefits, still involve costs of some magnitude.

---

*In *Where the Law Ends* Christopher Stone develops an extensive strategy of corporate reform that includes more than an expanded CSR, but CSR is a key element in his case for a diminution of government intrusion into business affairs.

CSR is based on the democratic premise that the American people should get what they want from the economic system, in the manner of a kind of citizen/consumer sovereignty. But given the dilemmas of benefits mixed with costs and likely trade-offs between the varied "goods" sought through business, rationality necessitates broad social evaluation of performance criteria and corporate behavior.

The argument here, in simple terms, is that data on what corporations are doing concerning social performance can facilitate this broad evaluation of associated benefits and costs. Information about what policies organizations are pursuing under the rubric of social responsibility can assist in shaping the rules of the economic game. For example, it can easily be a case of "social responsibility gone wild" if disclosure reveals that firms in assertive exercises of private power are sponsoring with stockholder money various political or social causes, left- or right-wing, that strike the fancy of some managers.

Consequently, CSR can aid in the inevitable public policy debate about the broad social requirements for U.S. business. This public policy process is necessarily ambiguous and controversial. But the supposition here is that disclosure about goals and practices can be a vital element in dialogue about the shape and character of the U.S. economy. What are particular firms and industries doing about employment of women and minorities? How does the pollution record of one industry compare with another? What are the trends over time in goals and results for consumer product safety? In what ways is due process at work in relationships of suppliers and dealers with manufacturing corporations? Information on these kinds of questions are an important ingredient in the broader public policy debate. Without it none of the participants have an empirically based understanding of how detailed benefits and costs of social requisites weigh out, of whether a truly optimal social policy concerning business is being approached.

Along with this extended discussion, a few brief remarks should be made about microlevel rationales for CSR. First, when corporations are assigned to perform in accordance with certain social goals, the challenge of carrying out those prescriptions falls to organizations' managerial staffs. In complex bureaucratic structures such as large corporations inevitably are, there is a considerable administrative gap between chief officers' enthusiastic commitment to minority employment or improved product safety, for example, and the consummation of those policies at operating levels. The "boss" in large organizations, even commercial ones, finds it difficult to see orders easily translated into operational behavior. It is naive to suppose that the president of a large company can say "jump" in a particular direction and expect an instantaneous reflex response throughout the enterprise. Inertia and both personal and divisional incentives often encourage the opposite course of action, with the politics of organization meaning that top managers standing alone have limited powers.

The management process requires communication, delegation, operational goal setting, monitoring and evaluation of results, and rewards for those effectively performing according to criteria elaborated by top management. To complete such a complex management process generally requires new structures and positions within the company—and new internal information systems to facilitate the monitoring and evaluation of results.

Many large corporations have responded to the evolving social climate with the staffing of consumer affairs, environmental, and fair employment offices, ge generally headed by vice-presidents. Their tasks include developing an expertise in social management and information systems applicable to social responsibility. These officers become part of the corporate staff, assisting divisional managers and their employees in carrying out goals elaborated by top corporate officers.

They are also involved in an integral way with monitoring and evaluating performance at the factory and office as they seek to give validity to the commitments stipulated by chief officers. It is apparent that an internal CSR system is essential to the successful accomplishment by complex organizations of society's performance criteria. An internal information system becomes part of the pedestrian but necessary managerial apparatus used to realize these expectations.

As a final element in the rationale for CSR, at the enterprise level managers wrestle with the allocation and budgeting dilemmas that grip all individuals or organizations with scarce resources. The core issue is to assign scarce resources in such a way as to maximize results for the firm. This challenge is present not only with manpower and capital inputs but also with allocations of social responsibility dollars. Obviously, calculation of benefit/cost ratios for such dollars is a formidable methodological undertaking, but CSR holds the promise of indicating at least the directions in which resources might be assigned for maximum return. For example, after making what it called an internal social-environmental audit, the First National Bank of Minneapolis concluded that its contribution dollars would have expanded benefits had they been reallocated away from cultural arts and toward improved housing, education, and employment.[4] With the same resources they could increase the "social responsibility bang for the buck" simply by reordering budget priorities. CSR at the microlevel can thus assist in this kind of allocative efficiency improvement.

The benefit/cost question, of course, extends to the proposition that CSR systems be introduced into large enterprises. In a sense what has been presented thus far explores the social and company benefits associated with CSR without any reference to costs. Perhaps on this count it is sufficient to note that a team of accounting experts on reports for corporate social performance conclude that the costs of instituting and maintaining such disclosure documents would be far below those associated with financial and other operational systems.[5] At this point the professional judgment of accounting specialists can be relied upon to give an approximation of the cost dimensions—and they conclude expenses are relatively modest.

It is apparent, moreover, that the cost of assembling information, which may be significant, must be matched with the cost of making decisions *without* information. This is perhaps at least part of the reverse side of the coin of informational benefits, the diminution in proportion of incorrect social and corporate choices as data is available. While it may appear that the costs of CSR are considerable, there is ample opportunity for such data developed as a by-product of reports already going to various government agencies. CSR does not need to start de novo with the collection of significant descriptions and data.

When it is all spelled out, it seems clear that the case for an external CSR both for internal purposes and external audiences is a strong and obvious one. The record of 85 percent of the *Fortune* 500 largest industrial corporations who now engage in some level of reporting of corporate social performance would indicate that it is a rationale accepted and understood by the managers of the nation's largest enterprises.

NOTES

1. For a careful, provocative analysis of the strengths and weaknesses of government control and of the market, see the landmark book by Christopher D. Stone, *Where the Law Ends: The Social Control of Corporate Behavior* (New York: Harper Colophon Books, 1975).

2. Reported in Phillip I. Blumberg, "The Public's 'Right to Know': Disclosure in the Major American Corporation," *The Business Lawyer*, July 1973, p. 1027, from Louis Brandeis, *Other People's Money* (National Home Library Edition, 1933), p. 62.

3. The cartoon is discussed in Christopher D. Stone, op. cit., p. 116. This paragraph and the following one, moreover, are based on Stone's cogent and significant analysis.

4. James L. Hetland, Jr., "The Social Audit: First National Bank's Experience," Address before the American Bankers Association, 1974 Public Affairs Conference, February 11, 1974, p. 9.

5. Arthur B. Toan, Jr., *The Measurement of Corporate Social Performance* (New York: American Institute for Certified Public Accountants, 1977), p. 290.

5

THE HISTORY AND ASSOCIATED DEVELOPMENTS OF CSR

In examining now CSR's history and background, the picture presented in Figure 5.1 is most valuable. It reminds us that financial accounting has developed over centuries, with the double-entry concept at least 200 years old; and it continues to evolve with advances in product-line and replacement-cost accounting contributions. To illustrate further the evolving character of accountability, a bare 50 years ago annual financial reports and related audits to stockholders were relatively rare occurrences. Prior to 1926, when the New York Stock Exchange first required annual reports, only 339 of 957 corporations made them available to shareholders.[1]

This "learning curve" of accountability also shows social accounting as a relative newcomer, an innovation of the 1970s. Historical depiction underlines the absurdity of expecting CSR to develop in a full fashion in the space of a decade or so. Accountability's historical development has been too lengthy to make that a likely prospect. What is seen now with CSR are early, crude versions of report structures. It will be the turn of the century, if ever, before widely accepted, fully developed information systems are devised. This is a sobering implication for enthusiasts and critics alike who expect an ideal information system in a few years. Some investigators critical of CSR apparently conclude that if a full system is not *now* universally in place it will never happen. The development process undoubtedly will be long.

As part of the historical record, however, there were interesting examples or suggestions of reporting on corporate social performance well before the 1970s. In 1940, as part of extensive congressional investigations of U.S. industry under the Temporary National Economic Committee (TNEC), Theodore Kreps,

FIGURE 5.1

Growth of Accountability Knowledge, 1775-1975

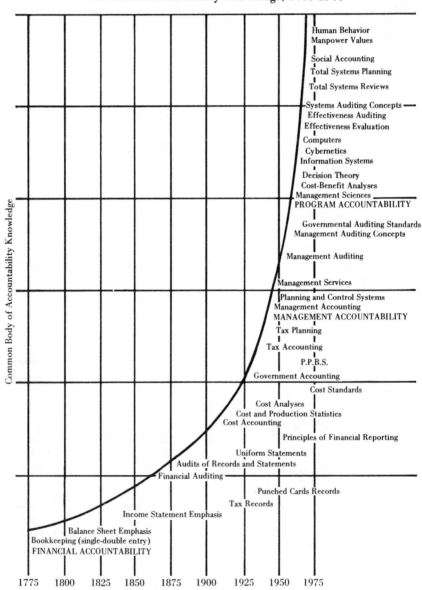

Source: Based on Claude S. Colantoni, W. W. Cooper, and H. J. Deitzer, "Accounting and Social Reporting," in Leo Herbert, "The Environment in Governmental Accounting in the Seventies," *The GAO Review* (Fall 1972), p. 31.

a noted economist at Stanford University, published a monograph entitled *Measurement of the Social Performance of Business*.[2] In this study, he used the term "social audit" well before Howard R. Bowen, who is thought to have coined the term, did in his important study *The Social Responsibilities of the Businessman*, published in 1953.[3]

Kreps'investigation concentrated on economic variables in evaluating 22 industries, nine industry groups, and three individual companies. However, this pioneer effort was an idea whose time had not yet come, for little more was done in terms of CSR for a period of 30 years. It does appear that in the 1970s social expectations and requirements for U.S. business make CSR a development resting not only on considerable preliminary work in related fields but also supported by wide business and social interest.

Some of the background pressures of demands for an accounting of corporate social performance and underlying quantitative social science analytical techniques are depicted in Figure 5.2. The pressures for social audits of business are related to trends dating from the 1930s; a variety of possible techniques for analysis and evaluation are available to CSR. CSR practitioners do not need to invent a range of techniques and procedures for description and analysis; a reasonable foundation already exists. CSR is interconnected with a variety of social science techniques.

More detail on the background and interrelated work of social measurement is given in Figure 5.3. CSR draws upon operations research, neoclassical economics, sociology, and political science, as well as accounting. The methodological background for an embryo corporate social accounting is based on these disciplines. Obviously, the intellectual challenge of developing a viable social accounting for corporate affairs is beset with difficulties. However, at least some of the exploratory work has been done in related fields. There is no guarantee of success in any short time frame for CSR, but some confidence for success does rest on the significance of earlier contributions. A key thing to remember also is that an elemental CSR already exists within most large U.S. corporations.

Contributors to CSR come from a diversity of backgrounds. To illustrate briefly this range of credentials and experience, operations research or management science is represented by the research of A. Charnes, W. W. Cooper, and Claude S. Colantoni; Neil Churchill and John Shank as accountant scholars have utilized Markov chains in evaluating affirmative action programs.[4] Broad social scientists, whose expertise is difficult to classify, have made noteworthy contributions; among them are Edward Bowman, Mason Haire, Raymond Bauer, Clark Abt, and Daniel Gray.[5] The work of accountant scholars is represented by that of Ralph Estes, Steven Dilley, Lee Seidler, David Linowes, and Marc Epstein.[6]

Economists researching in the field include John Tepper Marlin, Lee Preston, Albert Biderman, Joshua Ronen (whose expertise also includes accounting) and Meinholf Dierkes.[7] Even lawyers are engaged in analysis of the topic as reflected in the writings of David Ruder, Phillip I. Blumberg, Thomas Schoenbaum,

FIGURE 5.2

Background Pressures and Resources for CSR

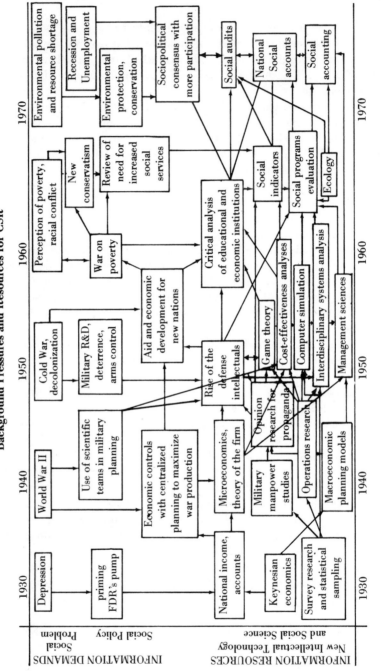

Source: Clark C. Abt, *The Social Audit for Management* (New York: Amacom, 1977), p. 217. Reprinted by permission.

FIGURE 5.3

Genealogy of Social Audits: The Four "Grandparent" Disciplines

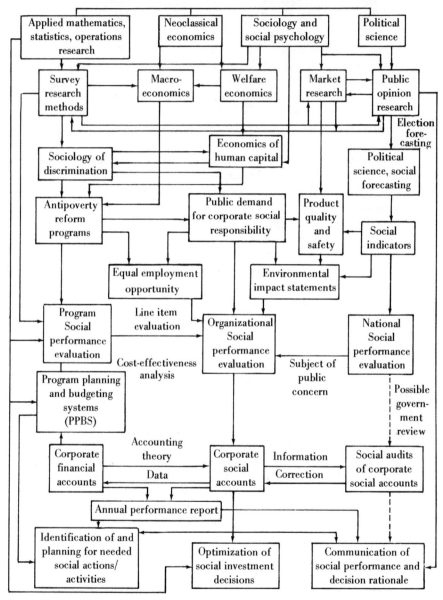

Source: Clark C. Abt, *The Social Audit for Management* (New York: Amacom, 1977), p. 218. Reprinted by permission.

Donald Schwartz, and Christopher D. Stone.[8] Students of business and society whose backgrounds are varied are another group of significant investigators, including George Steiner, Theodore V. Purcell, William Frederick, and Frederick Sturdivant.[9] This catalog of research is but a suggestive inventory, for the literature embraces a remarkable volume of effort.

Furthermore, development activity with CSR is not confined to U.S. practice and scholarship. There is growing interest and experience in companies in West Germany, Great Britain, Sweden, and France. Consultants and research institutes are at work, with a number of corporations publishing reports on social performance.[10] *L'Expansion*, a well-respected French business journal, for example, has on several occasions published studies of the social performance of leading corporations in that country.[11]

It is apparent from the interconnections depicted in the figures that two companion and potentially linked research efforts are presently under way, the first being in the area of macro or national social indicators. The purpose of these measures is to complement widely used economic categories of national income accounting. One approach of these efforts is to adjust GNP for various benefits and costs not captured by that concept, giving a one-dimensional adjusted estimate designated as Measure of Economic Welfare (MEW) or Net Economic Welfare (NEW).[12] An alternative approach to this measurement challenge is to devise a series of separate or multidimensional indicators of the state of society, including such aspects as public safety, health, education, income distribution, housing, and cultural advances.[13] Both of these alternatives are fueled by an apparent dissatisfaction with national income accounts as the sole gauge of social welfare or the "quality of life" in the United States.

Similarly, CSR reflects efforts to complement traditional financial measurements of the large business enterprises' performance with what are essentially *micro*social indicators, measures of social performance not at national or regional levels but within individual firms. At this stage in their separate developments there has been relatively little synergism or mutual interchange. However, it is revealing to see similar challenges and contrasting approaches to measurement in both areas. Some CSR researchers advocate a Tobin-Nordhaus one-dimensional technique, while others strongly defend the multidimensional alternative used for national social indicators. One point of interface, and there may be others, between macro- and micromeasures is with the physical and psychological quality of the work environment. Investigations are under way on this topic from both sides of the fence, from both macro- and microlevels of measurement.[14] Data on the subject appear in both kinds of reports. There is at least a potential for useful interchange.

To complete this background survey, two further aspects in the history of CSR must be discussed in order to explain why at the present moment disclosure is voluntary rather than required. During the 1960s and 1970s, with the rapid-fire passage of legislation dealing explicitly with the social performance of U.S. enterprise, detailed reports to federal agencies were required on such topics as equal and open employment, pollution, industrial accidents, deaths, and illnesses. It might be expected that this wealth of information relevant to key social expectations would be part of the public domain, open to all on an enterprise basis. The legislation could conceivably be a lever for full and thoroughgoing disclosure on social performance.

However, as part of the negotiations and "public policy process" involved with passage of the legislation, the laws provide for confidentiality at the firm level for data furnished to federal agencies. Thus, these laws have not served to shift CSR from voluntary to a required status.

Another possible avenue exists for the compulsory disclosure of data on social performance. The Security and Exchange Commission (SEC) has been under considerable pressure from various activist groups to require corporations under its jurisdiction to publish material relevant to CSR categories. The only movement in this direction, however, has been the stipulation that data on fair employment and pollution be published when such developments materially affect the firm's financial position. The SEC has concluded that its legislative mandate is to take into account the interests of investors, leaving to other agencies or Congress the disclosure needs of other corporate constituents.

The effect of these two circumstances is to put CSR on a voluntary basis, with corporate managers, if they desire, able to put a favorable construction on disclosures they choose to make. Social expectations frame CSR's broad outlines, but at present it can be a tool for either public relations or a balanced presentation of corporate strengths and shortcomings. However, it is also evident that present congressional requirements for confidentiality are not carved in stone. They are open to continuing public policy debate.

NOTES

1. W. C. Panord and W. P. Salzarulo, "Social Auditing: A Footnote of Full Disclosure," *Intellect*, November 1974, pp. 116-19.

2. See Archie B. Carroll and George W. Beiler, "Landmarks in the Evolution of the Social Audit," *Academy of Management Journal*, September 1975, pp. 589-99.

3. Howard R. Bowen, *Social Responsibilities of the Businessman* (New York: Harper, 1953).

4. See A. Charnes, Claude S. Colantoni, and W. W. Cooper, "Economic, Social and Enterprise Accounting and Mathematical Models," in J. Leslie Livingstone and S. C. Gunn, *Accounting for Social Goals: Budgeting and Analysis of Non Market Projects* (New York: Harper & Row, 1974); A. Charnes, W. W. Cooper, and G. Kozmetsky, "Measuring, Monitoring and Modeling Quality of Life," *Management Science*, June 1973; Neil Churchill and John Shank, "Accounting for Affirmative Action Programs," *Accounting Review*, October 1975.

5. See Edward Bowman and Mason Haire, "A Strategic Posture toward Corporate Social Reporting," *California Management Review*, Winter 1975; Raymond Bauer, a host of articles and books, including *The Corporate Social Audit*, Don H. Fenn, Jr., coauthor (New

York: AMACOM, 1977). Daniel Gray, "One Way to Go about Inventing Social Accounting," in Meinholf Dierkes and Raymond Bauer, *Corporate Social Accounting* (New York: Praeger, 1973).

6. See Ralph Estes, *Corporate Social Accounting* (New York: Wiley-Interscience, 1976); Steven Dilley, "External Reporting of Social Responsibility," *MSU Business Topics*, Autumn 1976; Lee J. Seidler and Lynn Seidler, *Social Accounting: Theory and Issues and Cases* (Los Angeles: Melville Publishing, 1975); David Linowes, *The Corporate Conscience* (New York: Hawthorn Books, 1974); Marc Epstein et al., *Corporate Social Performance: The Measurement of Product and Service Contributions* (New York: National Association of Accountants, 1977).

7. See John Tepper Marlin and Joseph H. Bragdon, Jr., "Is Pollution Profitable?" in *Risk Management*, April 1972, pp. 9-18; Lee E. Preston and J. E. Post, *Private Management and Public Policy: The Principle of Public Responsibility* (Englewood Cliffs, N.J.: Prentice-Hall, 1975); Albert D. Biderman and Thomas F. Drury, *Measuring Work Quality for Social Reporting* (New York: John Wiley, 1976); Joshua Ronen, "Accounting for Social Costs and Benefits," in Joe S. Cramer and Goerge Sorter, *Objectives of Financial Statements*, vol. 2 (New York: AICPA, 1974); Meinholf Dierkes and Raymond Bauer, *Corporate Social Accounting* (New York: Praeger, 1973).

8. See Phillip I. Blumberg, "The Public's Right to Know: Disclosure in the Major American Corporations," *The Business Lawyer*, July 1973; David S. Ruder, "Public Obligations of Private Corporations," *University of Pennsylvania Law Review*, 1965; Thomas J. Schoebaum, "The Relationship between Corporate Disclosure and Corporate Responsibility," *Fordham Law Review*, 1972; and Donald E. Schwartz, "Corporate Responsibility in the Age of Aquarius," *The Business Lawyer*, November 1970; and Christopher D. Stone, *Where the Law Ends: The Social Control of Corporate Behavior* (New York: Colophon Books, 1975).

9. See George Steiner and John J. Corson, *Measuring Business' Social Performance: The Corporate Social Audit* (New York: Committee for Economic Development, 1974); T. V. Purcell, "How G. E. Measures Managers in Fair Employment," *HBR*, November-December, 1974; William Frederick and James Blake, *Social Auditing* (New York: Praeger, 1977); Frederick D. Sturdivant, *Business and Society: A Managerial Approach* (Homewood, Ill.: Richard D. Irwin, 1977); and F. D. Sturdivant and James L. Ginter, "Corporate Social Responsiveness: Management Attitudes and Economic Performance," *California Management Review*, Spring 1977, pp. 30-39.

10. Dick Schaffer, "Time to Tot up a Social Audit," *The Accountant's Digest*, March 1976, pp. 175-76.

11. "L'Examen social 1976 des Entreprise Moyennes," *L'Expansion*, April 1976, pp. 94-121.

12. William Nordhaus and James Tobin, "Is Growth Obsolete?" *Economic Research: Retrospect and Prospect*, 50th Anniversary Colloquium 5 (New York: National Bureau of Economic Research, 1972; and Paul Samuelson, *Economics* (New York: McGraw-Hill, 1973), pp. 195-98.

13. U.S., Department of Health, Education and Welfare, *Toward a Social Report*, 1969; U.S., Executive Office of the President, Office of Management and Budget, *Social Indicators*, 1973.

14. See Albert D. Biderman and Thomas F. Drury, *Measuring Work Quality for Social Reporting* (New York: Wiley, 1976).

6

CSR TYPES, FORMATS, CONTENT, AND PROCEDURES

CSR is already accepted practice in most large corporations—at least to a preliminary and partial extent. It is instructive to examine the general features of this practice, and to study in some detail various proposals for strengthening and expanding social disclosure. This is the assignment at hand.

Table 6.1 summarizes typical patterns in external reporting by location and type of disclosure. The information, based on a 1974 survey of 250 annual reports, indicates a diversity in placement and kind. Monetary data and narrative presentations are most common; quantitative nonmonetary information are used somewhat infrequently. CSR is not often incorporated into financial statements but is generally found in separate annual report sections, in footnotes to financial statements, president's letters, or special reports to stockholders. Diversity in methods of reporting is the current pattern.

There are a multitude of explanations for such diversity; many factors give rise to variety in treatments. Differences in appraoch arise partly from the input-process-output characteristic of business operations. In simple terms, a wide set of inputs feed into the business "machine" coordinated by a management process, and outputs or results are generated. Some firms focus their reporting of social performance at the level of *inputs*, that is, how much is spent on pollution control projects. What is the size and distribution of the contributions budget? What are the *costs* of various programs? This kind of monetary information can readily be folded into existing financial documents or at least summarized in appropriate footnotes.

Other companies may decide to report on the effectiveness of the administrative process of social management. If it is a bank, how well are loan programs

TABLE 6.1

Categories of Social Performance Disclosure Appearing in Corporate Annual Reports

Placement of Disclosure	Type of Disclosure		
	Monetary	Quantitative (nonmonetary)	Narrative
Body of financial statements	Infrequent	Infrequent	Infrequent
Footnotes to financial statements	Relatively common	Infrequent	Relatively common
Letter to shareholders	Relatively common	Infrequent	Relatively common
Other section (such as a specially labeled, separate section, or comments in operating review sections of annual reports)	Relatively common	Relatively common	Relatively common

Source: Steven C. Dilley, "External Report of Social Responsibility," *M.S.U. Business Topics,* Autumn 1975, p. 14. Reprinted by permission of the publisher, Division of Research, Graduate School of Business Administration, Michigan State University.

to minority business administered? What is the relationship between program goals and achievements? This approach requires a more narrative kind of presentation easily placed in a special section of an annual report. The third and last possibility is disclosure of *outputs*, impacts, or social policy results. What is the shifting distribution of minority or female employment? What do surveys reveal about changing consumer attitudes concerning warranty policy, product safety, or consumer complaint systems? This aspect of business operations necessitates nonfinancial quantitative data in addition to narrative description. Different dimensions of the total business process prompt variation in *what* is reported on. Is it inputs to social performance, the quality or effectiveness of administrative policies and structures, or do reports relate to results and consequences?

Diversity within social disclosure also arises from different versions or models of reporting systems. Some researchers and companies propose extensive innovations in accounting structures, while others opt for limited extensions of existing practice. The general formats for organizing CSR can be categorized as follows: (1) a "big picture," new documents approach using "social" balance sheets and income statements; (2) an extension on existing practice and disclosure; (3) special reports, generally organized on a constituency basis; (4) rating schemes either on one aspect of business behavior or on overall company performance; or (5) program management appraisal. These approaches can be broadly characterized as "stock" or "balance sheet" efforts at measurement that examine behavior at a specific point in time. As will be seen, a sixth approach is available that concentrates on "flow," the process or trend of achieving particular goals. An exploration of each of these designs can give considerable insight into the current state of the CSR art.

"BIG PICTURE" INNOVATIONS

One useful way to characterize developments in social accounting is to distinguish between inventions and extensions.[1] The "big picture" contributions of Clark Abt,[2] David Linowes,[3] and Ralph Estes[4] fall clearly in the category of "inventions." It will be sufficient to survey the Estes and Abt versions to comprehend this alternative.

Ralph Estes is an accountant scholar who has done extensive work on CSR, recently elaborating a macroaggregate model for social accounting. It is a model based on the scheme depicted in Figure 6.1 and explained in more detail in Table 6.2. It is a proposed comprehensive model tallying up aggregate social benefits and costs of a corporation as they directly affect society, a familiar kind of structure to those aware of the positive and negative externalities concepts of economics. He leaves aside the perhaps insurmountable challenge of estimating the triggered, secondary, or indirect consequences of those direct impacts. Table 6.2 thus stands as an inventory of corporate activity's major social positive and negative effects.

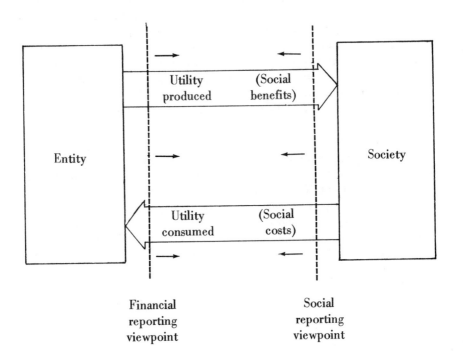

FIGURE 6.1

The Estes Social Performance Model of Reporting Viewpoints

$$SS = \sum_{i=1}^{n} \sum_{t=1}^{\infty} \frac{B_i}{(1+r)^t} \quad \sum_{j=1}^{m} \sum_{t=i}^{\infty} \frac{C_j}{(1+r)^t}$$

where SS = social surplus or deficit,
B_i = the ith social benefit,
C_j = the jth social cost,
r = an appropriate discount rate,
t = time period in which benefit or cost is expected to occur

Source: Ralph Estes, *Corporate Social Accounting* (New York: Wiley Interscience, 1976), pp. 93-94. Reprinted by permission.

A number of noteworthy characteristics of the Estes approach are apparent from perusal of his social impact statement. First, he seeks to subsume these diverse influences into the common denominator of dollars and cents. His is a one-dimensional approach to social disclosure. Second, as one social benefit he has the total value of products and services produced by the firm. This total value includes a "consumer surplus" that arises from the likely willingness of many buyers to pay more than they have to for given products. A social benefit of such magnitude is likely to swamp out many of the negatives of social costs estimated for his disclosure document. At any rate, recognition of the social benefit of the firm's production supports the proposition that a major business responsibility is to turn out desired goods and services. Finally, as with any balance sheet/income statement document it is possible structurally to calculate a net surplus or deficit flowing from the interchanges of a corporation and society.

The extraordinarily difficult task of assigning dollar values to the statement categories is approached with a variety of techniques already at least partially developed in the quantitative social sciences. For example, Estes would make considerable use in his measurement efforts of surrogate valuation and estimation of "shadow" prices for nonexistent market values. If a corporation loans building facilities to civic groups, an estimate of that social benefit would be the commercial rental value of similar property. Survey techniques devised for use with benefit/cost analysis are likewise a prominent weapon in the Estes arsenal. Restoration or avoidance cost can be used to estimate the impact of certain social disadvantages created by business. What would it cost to prevent or undo the damage? With some measurement problems a present value discounting procedure would be put to work as well as econometric manipulation of statistical data.

Estes offers a number of concrete examples of quantitative social science techniques to suggest that his model has some feasibility potential. He contends that many reasonable and operational techniques are available for estimating social benefits and costs. He reminds skeptics that financial and managerial accounting are full of estimation procedures and do not represent the stereotype of universal accuracy to the nearest penny. A demonstration of this is presented on how the total value of an enterprise's goods and services, including consumer surplus, might be calculated. Also, techniques for approximating the social costs of industrial injuries, accidents, and deaths are illustrated.

Each of these analytical procedures, however, conceals its own shortcomings and capabilities. In broad terms the Estes model is as strong as the quantitative measurement techniques of economics and other social sciences. An accounting team constructing an Estes social impact statement obviously would need to be skilled in the application of such investigative methods.

The Abt and Estes approaches to corporate social accounting are broadly similar though perhaps not in every detail. Estes sees CSR as useful for the social evaluation of business, while Abt stresses company benefits of more efficient management and resource allocation. Abt's construction can be viewed as an ap-

TABLE 6.2

The Estes Social Impact Statement for Progressive Company, Year Ended December 31, 19x1

Social benefits			$xxx
Products and services provided			
Payments to other elements of society			
Employment provided (salaries and wages)	$xxx		
Payments for goods and other services	xxx		
Taxes paid	xxx		
Contributions	xxx		
Dividends and interest paid	xxx		
Loans and other payments	xxx		
A Additional direct employee benefits		xxx	
Staff, equipment, and facility services donated		xxx	
Environmental improvements		xxx	
Other benefits		xxx	
T Total social benefits			$xxx
Social costs			
Goods and materials acquired		$xxx	
Buildings and equipment purchased		xxx	
Labor and services used		xxx	
Discrimination			
In hiring (external)	$xxx		
In placement and promotion (internal)	xxx		
Work-related injuries and illness		xxx	
Public services and facilities used		xxx	

Other resources used   xxx

Environmental damage

Terrain damage	$xxx
Air pollution	xxx
Water pollution	xxx
Noise pollution	xxx
Solid waste	xxx
Visual and aesthetic pollution	xxx
Other environmental damage	xxx xxx

Payments from other elements of society	
Payments for goods and services provided	$xxx
Additional capital investment	xxx
Loans	xxx
Other payments received	xxx xxx

Other costs   xxx

Total social costs   xxx

Social surplus (deficit) for the year $xxx

Accumulated surplus (deficit) December 31, 19x0   xxx

Accumulated surplus (deficit) December 31, 19x1 $xxx

Notes:

1. Significant indirect effects associated with inputs.
2. Significant indirect effects associated with outputs.
3. Bases for measurements and estimates.
4. Progress in areas of current societal concern (such as environmental protection outlays and activities, employment and promotion of minorities and women, and energy conservation efforts).

Source: Ralph Estes, *Corporate Social Accounting* (New York: Wiley-Interscience, 1976), pp. 96-97. Reprinted by permission.

plication of the Estes model, as is apparent in Table 6.3. Both want the rather broad measures of social benefits and costs translated into monetary values and contend that reasonable estimation procedures for market values are available or can be developed. As is evident in Table 6.3, however, Abt seeks an integration of financial and social documents into a single presentation.

Abt's work preceded that of Estes chronologically. Abt has been a leading and pioneer researcher in CSR; his efforts have evoked both respect and controversy. He has generated actual social balance sheets and income statements using analytical procedures discussed by Estes. Table 6.3 depicts a combined social and financial statement, with accompanying footnotes spelling out the general methods used in calculating estimates. They demonstrate that there is method to Abt's estimation madness.

He suggests there are many public studies of cost effectiveness and benefit/cost analysis with education, health, and pollution; these are valuable resources for individuals developing methods for the disclosure of corporate social performance. A major feature of his measurement techniques is to estimate the "market worth" of the social benefits and costs of corporate activity. He uses opportunity-cost estimation to get at market values when none exist. For example, in approximating the social cost of foul-smelling air associated with a factory, he calculates the market value of nonfoul atmosphere. This can be done by comparing differentials in real estate values when the influence of all other factors has been held constant in statistical analysis. Once the estimate of clear air value is calculated as an opportunity cost associated with the air pollution, it is multiplied by the population affected by the offending factory to obtain a relevant social cost approximation. A careful examination of his statement footnotes indicates other general methods used.

A few comments can be offered in brief appraisal of these techniques. The Abt invention in social accounting has both been widely criticized and acclaimed as a daring attempt at social accounting. It is important to see that neither it nor the Estes model originates from out of the blue; analytically, it rests on fairly standard social science approaches. It is an effort at applying procedures at the micro or firm level usually employed with aggregate data and broad social problems. Nonetheless, this does not mean that either Abt or Estes has come upon foolproof techniques. It simply helps explain what their approach involves.

Their estimates are not purely judgmental, though the level of objectivity is not as great as Abt would argue. Complete Abt-Estes versions have not been completed with organizations other than the Abt management consulting firm, where the task might be easier than with multiproduct, divisional corporations. Clearly, however, this is a line of research and practice that should be developed, though it is not the likely form of CSR for the near future. CSR as actually pursued by American business has been much more pedestrian, partial, and selective than these "big picture" models of social performance measurement.

TABLE 6.3

Social and Financial Income Statement, Abt Associates, Inc., 1974, 1975
(in thousands of dollars)

Suppliers of Social Resources	Social Benefits — are social or economic resources that are generated by company operations and have a positive impact or add to society's resources			Social Costs — are social or economic resources that are consumed by company operations and are a cost sacrifice or detriment to society			Net Social Income* — or social profit is the social gain or loss to society resources that result from company operations	
	Note	1975	1974	Note	1975	1974	1975	1974
Company/stockholders								
Contract revenue	17	15,806	16,423					
Federal services consumed	18	253	262					
State services consumed	19	95	104					
Local services consumed	20	42	40					
Pollution to the environment								
Caused by company operations	21							
Generation of electricity	22	55	37					
Staff commuting	23	19	21					
Paper consumed	24	7	7					
Dividends	25	74	59					
Salaries paid (exclusive of training investment and fringe benefits)				26	5,707	5,296		
Training investment in staff				27	766	935		
Direct contract cost				28	4,298	5,529		
Overhead/general administrative expenditures not itemized				29	1,823	1,796		
Vacation and holidays				30	763	719		
Improvements in space and environment				31	127	137		
Federal taxes paid				32	462	474		
State taxes paid				32	109	130		
Local taxes paid				32	118	78		
Health, dental, and life insurance				33	252	256		
Sick leave				34	185	185		
Staff food service				35	73	67		
Child care facilities				36	26	18		
Tuition reimbursement				37	23	15		
Employee stock ownership plan				38	30	0		
Interest payments				39	267	197		
Income foregone on paid-in capital				40	306	265		
Social audit development				41	4	14		
Retirement income plan				42	118	50		
Total company stockholder benefits		16,351	16,953					
Total company/ stockholders equity					15,457	16,161		
Total company/ stockholders equity (note 43)							894	792

(continued)

61

TABLE 6.3 *(continued)*

Suppliers of Social Resources	Social Benefits *are social or economic resources that are generated by company operations and have a positive impact or add to society's resources*	Note	1975	1974	Social Costs *are social or economic resources that are consumed by company operations and are a cost sacrifice or detriment to society*	Note	1975	1974	Net Social Income* *or social profit is the social gain or loss to society resources that result from company operations*	Note	1975	1974
Staff (note 44)	Salaries paid for time worked	45	6,473	6,231	Opportunity cost of total time worked	59	7,509	7,540				
	Career advancement	46	758	700	Absence of retirement income plan	60	0	1				
	Vacation and holidays	47	763	719	Layoffs and involuntary terminations	61	115	77				
	Health, dental, and life insurance	48	454	461	Inequality of opportunity	62	1	1				
	Sick leave	49	185	185	Uncompensated losses through theft	63	1	1				
	Retirement income plan	50	118	50	Reduced parking area	64	0	29				
	Employee stock ownership plan	51	30	0								
	Staff food service	52	73	67								
	Parking	53	121	95								
	Quality of work space	54	122	134								
	Tuition reimbursement	55	23	15								
	Child care facility	56	26	18								
	Credit union	57	16	11								
	Recreation center	58	35	27								
	Total staff benefits		9,197	8,713	Total staff cost		7,626	7,649	Total staff equity		1,571	1,064
Clients/ general public	Value of contract research	65	15,806	16,423	Cost of contract work to clients	70	15,806	16,423				
	Staff overtime worked but not paid	66	1,036	1,184	Federal services consumed	71	253	262				
	Federal taxes paid	67	462	474	State services consumed	71	95	104				
	State and federal tax worth of net jobs created	68	25	96	Pollution to the environment Caused by company operations	72						
	State taxes paid	67	109	130	Generation of electricity	22	55	37				
	Contribution to knowledge	69	72	60	Staff commuting	23	19	21				
					Paper consumed	24	7	7				
	Total client benefits		17,510	18,367	Total cost to clients		16,235	16,854	Total client equity		1,275	1,513
Community	Local taxes paid	73	118	78	Increased parking area	77	3	0				
	Local tax worth of net jobs created	74	4	16	Local services consumed	78	42	40				
	Environmental improvements	75	29	36								
	Reduced parking area	76	0	29								
	Total community benefits		151	159	Total cost to community		45	40	Total community equity		106	119
	Total	79	43,209	44,192	Total		39,363	40,704	Total (note 80)		3,846	3,488

62

*Net social income is a social dividend paid out to company/stockholders, staff, clients/general public, or community, and it does not accrue to the net social worth on the balance sheet.

Notes:

17. Valuation of contract revenue is based upon the total revenue from the 1975 and 1974 income statements.

18. Federal services consumed by the company are calculated by multiplying the ratio of company revenues to total U.S. corporate revenue times the total U.S. corporate tax collections. Federal services consumed average about 1.59 percent of total company revenue over the past four years. *Source:* Survey of Current Business, U.S. Department of Commerce.

19. State services consumed by the company are calculated by multiplying the ratio of company revenue to the State of Massachusetts corporate revenue times the total State of Massachusetts corporate tax collections. State services consumed average about 0.6 percent of the company's revenue over the past five years.

20. The company's share of local services consumed is computed by multiplying the ratio of the average daily work force of the company to the local population by total local taxes collected and subtracting the percentage of the local community budget going to education. Local services consumed average about 0.65 percent of total salaries paid for time worked (note 45).

21. In its operations, the company contributes to the degradation of environmental resources through pollution. The cost of pollution abatement is treated as a benefit to the company and a cost to society.

22. The company consumed 2,731,000 kwh of electric power in 1975 and 1,831,000 kwh in 1974. The cost of abate-

ment of air pollution created by the production of this power is estimated at $.02 per kwh.

23. The company generated 1,894,464 commuting trip miles in 1975 and 2,079,450 miles in 1974 (4,784 and 4,037 per staff member). The cost of abatement of air pollution caused by automobile commuting is estimated at $.01 per mile.

24. The company used 212 tons of paper in 1975 and 200 tons in 1974. The cost of abatement of water pollution created by the manufacture of this paper is estimated at $35 per ton.

25. The company paid dividends of $74,000 in 1975 and $59,000 in 1974, which are treated as benefit to the stockholders and added for the first time this year.

26. Salaries paid exclusive of training investment and fringe benefits are valued at total salaries earned by staff (1975: $6,473,000 and 1974: $6,231,000) less training investment (note 27).

27. Training investment in staff is a social cost to the company and stockholders because time spent in training is not billable to contracts and results in less profit per staff member. The staff survey indicates the amount of time staff spent in training and these percentages have been applied to total salaries for time worked (note 26) to delineate training investment.

28. Figures taken from 1975 and 1974 financial income statement.

29. Figures taken from 1975 and 1974 financial income statement and adjusted for

itemized expenditures. The 1974 amount shown on the 1974 statement has been changed from $1,860,000 to $1,796,000 because social audit development and retirement income plan are now shown as itemized expenditures (notes 41 and 42).

30. Vacation and holiday is part of the annual payroll for time worked and is valued at its cost to the company.

31. Actual expenditures on building maintenance are a social and economic cost to the company and stockholders.

32. Federal, state, and local taxes paid by the company represent social and economic cost because they result in a direct loss of funds to the company. Valuation is based upon cost to the company.

33. The cost of health, dental, and life insurance purchased for staff is assumed to be equal to its cost to the company.

34. Sick leave is part of the annual payroll for time worked and its cost is assumed to be equal to its cost to the company.

35. Valuation of staff food service is assumed to be equal to its cost to the company of $47,000 for food and coffee provided and $26,000 for the value of space given up to provide eating facilities (4,000 sq. ft. at $6.50).

36. Valuation of child care facility is based on its cost to the company of $26,000 for food and other miscellaneous services.

37. Valuation of tuition reimbursement is equal to its cost to the company.

38. Valuation of employee stock ownership plan is assumed to be equal to its

cost to the company of $30,000 in 1975.

39. Interest payments are a social and economic cost to the company and stockholders because the amount spent to borrow money cannot be used for other purposes. Social cost is equal to the amount actually spent during the year.

40. Income foregone on paid-in capital is the opportunity cost to stockholders of having equity (beginning 1975: $3,166,000 and beginning 1974: $2,698,000) tied up in the company. The opportunity cost is equivalent to the expected return on investment in a medium-risk venture (estimated at 12 percent) less dividends paid during the year (1975: $74,000 and 1974: $59,000).

41. Valuation of social audit development is equal to its cost to the company during the year.

42. Employee retirement income plan was started as a new staff benefit in 1974. Its social cost to the company is equal to amounts spent on the plan by the company each year.

43. The 1974 net benefits for stockholders was restated because of the addition of dividends to stockholders (note 25).

44. Total number of employees increased from 519 in 1974 to 536 in 1975 and these numbers are reflected in the totals reported in the social and financial income statements.

45. Salaries paid for time worked is valued at the total amount of pay staff receive for time worked during the year. Average salary per employee was $12,076 in 1975 and $12,005 in 1974.

46. Career advancement is equated to the added earning power from salary increases for

(continued)

TABLE 6.3 (continued)

merit or promotion. The annualized salary increases (monthly amount times 12) was $758,000 in 1975 and $700,000 in 1974. Average increase per employee was $1,414 in 1975 and $1,348 in 1974.

47. Vacation and holidays is a social benefit to the staff valued at its dollar cost to the company, which resulted in a benefit per employee of $1,423 in 1975 and $1,385 in 1974.

48. The value of health, dental, and life insurance provided by the company is assumed to be equal to the cost of purchasing comparable coverage individually by full-time staff. For each dollar spent, the company generates $1.80 of benefits per employee. Benefits per employee amounted to $847 in 1975 and $888 in 1974.

49. Sick leave is a social benefit to the staff assumed to be equal to its cost to the company. Benefits per employee were $345 in 1975 and $356 in 1974.

50. The value of the retirement income plan is equal to the cost of purchasing the plan by the company. Benefits per employee were $220 in 1975 and $192 in 1974.

51. The employee stock ownership plan is a new benefit to staff that is valued at its cost to the company.

52. Staff food service is a social benefit to the staff valued at its cost to the company (note 35). Benefits per employee were $136 in 1975 and $129 in 1974.

53. Free parking is offered to all employees and is a social benefit to staff valued at the estimated savings in terms of alternative locations. Free parking privileges are assumed to be worth $30 per month and the number of parking spaces increased from 150 in 1974 to 222 in 1975. Benefits per employee were $225 in 1975 and $183 in 1974.

54. The value of the quality of work space the company provides employees is estimated to be the amount of floor space per staff (125 sq. ft. in 1975 and 130 sq. ft. in 1974) exceeding industry standards (average of 90 sq. ft per employee). The value of actual square footage in excess of industry standards is estimated at $6.50/sq. ft. As a result of company employment growth, the average benefit per employee has decreased from $258 in 1974 to $227 in 1975.

55. Valuation of tuition reimbursement as a benefit to staff is based on the cost to the company (note 37). Average benefits per employee were $42 in 1975 and $28 in 1974.

56. The value of social benefits the child care center provides to the staff is equal to the cost to the company (note 36). Average benefits per employee were $48 in 1975 and $34 in 1974.

57. The value of social benefits the credit union provides to the staff (in the form of lower interest rates for loans and higher dividends for deposits) is measured at its cost to the company for resources contributed such as staff salaries (1975: 15,000 and 1974: $10,000) and floor space and other services (1975: $1,000 and 1974: $1,000).

58. Recreation center membership is offered to all employees and is a social benefit to the staff valued at the estimated saving members receive in terms of alternative membership in swimming and tennis clubs. Saving per member is estimated to be $225 per year. In 1975 there were 157 staff memberships compared to 120 in 1974.

59. Opportunity cost of total time worked is a social cost to the staff because it represents total time given up by the staff while working for the company. The value of this cost to society is equal to the total salaries received for regular working hours (1975: $6,473,000 and 1974: $6,231,000) plus the value of overtime

worked but not paid (1975: $1,036,000 and 1974: $1,184,000). Average cost per employee was $14,009 in 1975 and $14,527 in 1974.

60. Absence of retirement plan is a social cost to the four employees who would have had a vested interest (present value of benefits is estimated to be $1,000), but terminated before the retirement plan began on July 1, 1974.

61. Layoffs and involuntary terminations are social costs to the staff. A survey of terminees indicates that 45 percent were still unemployed after 60 days, therefore, the social cost is estimated to be one month's salary at time of termination (1975: $1,140 and 1974: $736) for the terminees who found employment within 60 days (1975: 39 and 1974: 40) and two months' salary for the terminees who found work after 60 days (1975: 31 and 1974: 32). The average cost per staff was $213 in 1975 and $148 in 1974.

62. Inequality of opportunity is a social cost to the staff valued at the cost to individuals of the income loss equal to the difference between what the minority individual or female earns and what a nonminority or male individual doing the same job with the same qualifications earns. The social cost of inequality of opportunity has remained constant at $1,000 in 1975 and 1974.

63. Uncompensated loss through theft of staff personal property is a social cost to the staff because of the loss suffered for which they were not reimbursed. The loss has remained constant at $1,000 in 1975 and 1974 after the establishment of security measures.

64. Reduction in parking area in 1974 was a cost to the staff valued at $30 a month for the 80 parking spaces no longer available for staff usage. Parking was increased in 1975 so that the cost to the staff was reduced to zero.

65. Contract research is a benefit to the client and society because it is the primary output of company operations. The value of the benefit is assumed to be equal to the price that the client paid to have the work done (1975: $15,806,000 and 1974: $16,423,000) since this represents the fair market value or cost of the research. A survey of clients indicated that the evaluation of contract values at cost to the client understates the true value to the public of the work performed by the company. However, the available data is not reliable enough to be used to estimate the actual value of the research.

66. The total value of overtime worked and not paid for is a social benefit provided to the client and the general public by the company staff. The 1975 staff survey showed a decrease of overtime to 16 percent of regular working hours ($6,473,000) from 19 percent of regular working hours ($6,231,000) in 1974.

67. Federal and state taxes paid by the company are a social and economic benefit to the general public and their benefit is valued at their cost to the company.

68. Federal and state tax worth of net jobs created are a social benefit to the general public because each new job will create additional tax revenue. Expansion of the company has created 17 net new jobs in 1975 as compared to 67 in 1974. The tax value of these additional jobs for the federal and state governments is computed as 20 percent of the average starting salary of $12,000 weighted by the proportion of a full year that these net new jobs have been effective (note 62).

69. Contribution to knowledge is a social benefit to the general public because publications by the company staff constitute additions to the stock of knowledge. These publications are valued at the average market rate for similar publications, which is estimated to be $4,000 for the 18 technical publications in 1975.

70. Cost of contract research is a social cost to the client (federal and state governments) because payment to the company reduces the amount of money available for other purposes and therefore represents a direct cost to society. It is valued at the amount paid to the company (1975: $15,806,000 and 1974: $16,423,000).

71. Federal and state services consumed are social cost to the general public and society because of the company's use of public services that flow from the federal and state governments. See notes 18 and 19 for method of measurement for services consumed.

72. Pollution to the environment caused by the company's operation is a social cost to the general public and society caused by the company operation and not paid for. Valuation of these costs to the client can be found in notes 21, 22, and 23.

73. Local taxes paid by the company are a social benefit to the local community and are valued at their cost to the company.

74. Local tax worth of net jobs created are a social benefit to the local community because each new job will create additional tax revenue. Expansion of the company has created 17 net new jobs in 1975, a decrease from 67 in 1974. Additional revenue to the local community are in terms of sales taxes, excise taxes, and real estate taxes estimated to be 3.2 percent of the average starting salary of $12,000, weighted by the proportion of the years that the jobs have been in effect (note 62).

75. Environmental improvements are a direct, visible social benefit to the local community that are valued at their cost to the company. In 1975 the company spent $29,000 on landscaping, a decrease from $36,000 in 1974.

76. Reduction in parking area in 1974 was a social benefit to the local community because it reduced pollution, traffic, and other social problems associated with automobiles. However, the parking area was increased during 1975 so that there was no social benefit to the community in 1975.

77. Increase in parking area in 1975 (72 spaces) was a social cost to the local community because of increased automobile usage during the year. The value of this cost is estimated at the amount of pollution caused by 72 automobiles commuting an average of 18.4 miles per day and the cost of abatement of air pollution estimated at $.01 per mile (1975: $3,000).

78. Local services consumed are a social cost to the local community because use of these services by the company reduces the amount of services available for others in the community. See note 20 for details on the calculation of this cost to the local community.

79. Total social benefit for 1974 has been increased from $44,133,000 (note 25).

80. Total net social benefit for 1974 has been increased from $3,429,000 (notes 25, 43, and 79).

Source: Based on Clark C. Abt, *The Social Audit for Management* (New York: Amacom, 1977), pp. 258-64.

EXTENSIONS ON EXISTING REPORTING SYSTEMS

Three examples are sufficient to illustrate the proposition that CSR need not involve extraordinary innovations with accounting documents. Relatively modest footnotes and new account schemes or expansions based on existing statements can make available useful information for internal planning or corporate constituencies.

In traditional accounting practice, the social costs of business activity are note an easily distinguished part of a firm's books. That being the case, companies interested in meeting social expectations are by the standards of usual accounting practice at a disadvantage. If they seek to shift those costs from society or particular impacted groups to the corporation by increased pollution control expenditures or expanded factory safety efforts, for example, they will be at a competitive cost disadvantage. In the absence of legislation or reporting revisions that recognize the fact of social costs flowing from the firm, an industry may be forced into the deplorable position of avoiding social costs generated by their production. Firms seeking to internalize such costs find it difficult and probably impossible to lead the way to better practice.

As discussed earlier, violations of laws and norms sooner or later are likely to affect company financial performance adversely. Fines, damages arising from court suits, or stringent legislation in the future may be the outcomes of lowest common denominator performance. As a likely case in point, having dismissed the external repercussions of heavy highway fatalities, pollution, repair bills, and growing dependence on pollution in the 1950s and 1960s, the automobile industry is now forecast to reap much lower profits in the 1980s than in the past.[5]

To reduce the dilemma of this kind of freeloading trap for industry, Floyd Beams and Paul Fertig have proposed a technically modest way of accounting for the social costs of enterprise. By introducing accrual/deferred liability elements into the record the costly practices of internalizing negative diseconomies would be matched on the books of laggard competitors with a full reporting of costs postponed for the future.[6] Reserves that recognize social costs experienced in the past, present, or future could also be established.

At least a tentative step in this direction is apparent in the footnoting to the Ansul Company's 1974 annual report, shown in Table 6.4. The note describes a waste disposal reserve anticipated for future pollution costs. To be sure, the information in the note is sparse and should be expanded to include more data and narrative about this aspect of corporate social performance, but it indicates how a contingent liability approach to CSR can be conducted. The thrust of recent SEC requirements concerning social costs associated with pollution and fair employment encourages a recognition of the firm's contingent liabilities.

Illustrations of more thoroughgoing extensions on existing reporting documents are depicted in Tables 6.5 and 6.6. Claude S. Colantoni, W. W. Cooper, and H. J. Deitzer, all of Carnegie-Mellon University, propose that a relatively sim-

TABLE 6.4

Excerpt from the Ansul Company 1974 Annual Report: Notes to Consolidated Financial Statements

Note 7—Stock Option Plan. Under the 1966 Management Employee Qualified Stock Option Plan, options have been granted to certain officers and key employees to purchase shares of common stock at 100 percent of fair market value on the date of grant. Options become exercisable as to 50 percent of the optioned shares during the second year after grant and the balance during the third year. All options terminate five years after grant.

Stock Option Transactions Were as Follows:	Number of Shares	Average Price per Share (dollars)
Outstanding January 1, 1973	83,033	9.57
Changes during 1973		
Granted	7,946	11.28
Terminated	(7,831)	14.21
Exercised	(1,523)	8.98
Outstanding December 31, 1973	81,625	9.31
Changes during 1974		
Granted	8,072	14.20
Terminated	(600)	12.13
Exercised	(12,175)	9.22
Outstanding December 31, 1974	76,922	9.82
(1973 adjusted for 4 percent stock dividend in 1974)		

At December 31, 1974, 66,229 shares (50,216 at December 31, 1973) under option were exercisable and 10,147 shares (17,678 at December 31, 1973) were available for grant.

Note 8—Deferred Items. Deferred items at December 31, 1974 and 1973 were as follows:

	1974 (dollars)	1973 (dollars)
Deferred currency exchange gains	740,369	1,137,595
Waste disposal reserve	1,915,000	1,000,000
Total	2,655,369	2,137,595

The waste disposal reserve has been provided for anticipated costs that may be associated with the recycling or disposal of a salt waste by-product of our domestic agricultural chemical production. During 1974, we determined that any recycling or disposal program probably will be completed over a period of time exceeding one year. As a result we have classified the waste disposal reserve and related future tax benefits as noncurrent items. The December 31, 1973 balance sheet and statement of changes in financial position have been restated to conform with the 1974 classifications.

Source: Steven C. Dilley, "External Reporting of Social Responsibility," *MSU Business Topics*, Autumn 1975, p. 18. Reprinted by permission of the publisher, Division of Research, Graduate School of Business Administration, Michigan State University.

TABLE 6.5

A Hypothetical Income Statement Extended to Include Environmental Variables Expenditures
(dollars per ton[a])

| | | Employee Costs | | Expenses | | | | | Net Income |
	Revenues	Wages	Benefits	Consumption	Depreciation	Interest	Taxes	Net Income	per Share[b]
Gross financial and economic income									
Total revenues and expenses (without programs) (dollars in millions)	4,929	1,767	352	2,092	229	57	205	227	—
Revenues and expenses per ton of output (without programs)	204.54	73.32	14.61	86.80	9.50	2.38	8.50	9.43	11.34
Social environment									
Housing investment = $75 million investment	0.31	—	0.12	0.15	0.30	0.27	(0.25)	(0.28)	(0.325)
Minority employment = 15 percent of work force	—	1.25	.20	.30	1.00	—	(1.25)	(1.50)	(1.80)
OSHA Index < 75	—	.08	.02	.05	—	—	—	0.00	0.00
Manpower training = 200 people per year	.15	—	—	—	—	—	—	—	—
High school equivalency training = 300 employees	—	—	—	—	—	—	—	—	—
Summer jobs for needy youth = 800 per year	—	.10	—	—	—	—	—	(.10)	(.12)
Physical environment									
Sulfur removal to 98 level = $300 million investment	1.00	0.25	0.05	0.70	1.20	0.95	(1.00)	(1.15)	(1.385)
Noise abatement program	—	—	—	—	—	—	—	—	—
Net financial and economic income									
Total revenues and expenses (net of programs) (dollars in millions)	4,960	1,835	356	2,102	290	74	149	154	7.70
Revenues and expenses per ton of output (net of programs)	206.00	75.00	15.00	88.00	12.00	3.60	6.00	6.40	—

[a] Calculated on the basis of a total output of 24.1 million tons.
[b] Based on 20 million shares of common stock.

Notes:

1. This display is the budgeted income statement for the firm. It not only provides the aggregate financial information in the same fashion as it would in a traditional income statement but also includes other flow information for various socially oriented programs.

2. The aggregate flow information is provided under the title "Gross financial and economic income." The first line represents the actual dollar flow in millions while the second is the dollar flow per unit of physical output. The latter measure may involve only the product of greatest output or may be some value such as a weighted average of output levels, for example. However, once a value is chosen it must be used consistently in displaying all the data. In this case, the choice is 24.1 million tons of output, where output is measured in terms of sales rather than in terms of such other bases as production, and the like. Although some of these latter bases might provide better measures for some purposes, their use would lead into a discussion of their capitalization and related issues that we should prefer to avoid. In this case, we want to deal only with costs that we can treat as "period" costs, rather than with those that must be capitalized into inventory for distribution at subsequent periods. If some other basis were found to be preferable, some adjustment would have to be made to these figures to account for increases or decreases in inventory levels.

3. In an attempt to meet housing needs in a depressed area near a plant, the firm in question decided to invest $75 million in the design, engineering, and construction of a 3,000-unit, multiple-family dwelling. Rental income or revenue is assumed to be $2,500 per unit per year or $.31 per ton of output. Although the housing units can be rented by anyone in the area, employees can rent these facilities at 60 percent of the prevailing rental rate in this area; the company treats the remaining 40 percent as an employee benefit. The total amount treated by the company as employee benefits converts to $.12 per ton of output. Operating costs amount to $.15 per ton of output for the year. Accelerated depreciation is scheduled over the 20-year life of this investment through the sale of bonds. The tax expense is a negative $.25 per ton of output because the project operates at a loss to the company. The net impact of this project on net income per ton of output is $.28, for a total loss of $6.75 million.

4. In order to allow minority groups to participate more fully in its labor markets, the firm will undertake recruiting and job expansion programs aimed directly at minorities. It is expected that this will raise the employment level of these groups to 15 percent from current levels of 8 percent, with a resultant 2 percent net increase in total employment.

5. The Occupational Safety and Health Act of 1970 set standards for health and safety performance in manufacturing and administrative units. Compliance with the law requires that an index measure of this firm's behavior be at 100. However, the current index value is 75 and therefore additional outlays are required. Costs delineated for this program are incremental above those that are incurred to provide compliance with the law.

6. The manpower training program administered by this firm provides vocational training to 200 people per year. The skills they acquire are highly specialized and yield compensation sufficient to insure a middle-income standard of living. Most of these people are employed by other firms—some of them competitors—upon completion of their training. The program is fully funded by the federal government.

7. Many of the company's unskilled laborers have not had an opportunity to complete their high school training. For these people the company sponsors fully funded high school courses that take place after working hours. Upon successful completion of this program, the participants receive a high school equivalence diploma. Three hundred employees are currently enrolled in this program.

8. High school students over 16, who qualify on the basis of need, are eligible for participation in summer employment programs. It is expected that 800 of these youth will be employed in the next year. Their wages are treated as a direct expense.

9. In order to comply with proposed regulations governing sulfur emissions, it is expected that capital equipment worth $50 million will be installed. A slight increase in revenues is anticipated from by-product credits and the higher price that the purer product will then warrant. Present expenses, however, are considerably higher; thus, the treatment of the entire cost of compliance as a period charge results in an overall money loss.

10. In the next year the firm will begin a noise abatement program within the factory for which only expenses related to the preliminary plans have been incurred to date. To employees and neighbors the realized plan should provide quieter surroundings and better health. It is also expected that continued operation of the proposed program for noise abatement will have a positive effect on productivity over time, but neither the magnitude nor the timing of these productivity increases can be assessed at present. Thus, all of the costs to date are being expensed as a period charge.

Source: Claude S. Colantoni, W. W. Cooper, and H. J. Deitzer, "Budgeting Disclosure and Social Accounting," in *Corporate Social Accounting*, ed. Meinholf Dierkes and Raymond Bauer (New York: Praeger, 1973), pp. 370-71.

TABLE 6.6

A Multidimensional Income Statement for Corporate Social Reporting
(millions of dollars)

Traditional Net Income Statement		External Payments	Physical Environment			Social Environment				
			Sulfur Emissions (million pounds)	Sulfur Removal	Particulate Emissions (million pounds)	Employment (number of workers in thousands)	OSHA Index (worker accident days lost)	Black Female Participation (in percentages)	Manpower Training (in workers)	Corporate-Owned Housing (in units)
Net sales	4,600			24.1						
Less: cost of goods sold beginning inventory	840									
Plus: manufacturing costs										
Labor: wages	1,440	1,440		6.0						
Benefits	360	360		1.2		144	216	9.1	1,600	2,100
Materials	1,725	1,725		16.9						
Depreciation	225	452*		28.9						(75)
Total manufacturing	3,750		50		35					
Goods available	4,590									
Less: engineering inventory	923									
Total cost of goods sold	3,667									
Gross margin	933									
Less: selling and administration			1		2					
Salaries	352	352				36	2	0.9	400	150
Benefits	88	88						10.3		35
Materials and supplies	420	420								
Depreciation	56									
Net operating income	17									
Plus: other income	360									

Income before distribution	—	377	—	—	—	—	—	—	—	—	—
Less: distributions											
Interest	74	—	74	—	—	—	—	—	—	—	—
Taxes	149	—	149	—	22.8	—	—	—	—	—	—
Dividends	97	320	97	—	(24.1)	—	—	—	—	—	—
Net income transferred to ac-cumulated undistributed earnings	—	57	5,157	51	(27.6)	37	180	218	7.5	3.8	2,000	2,210

*Net purchases of plant and equipment.

Notes:

1. All items in the "Traditional Net Income Statement" column are values expressed in millions of dollars. The statement is prepared in accordance with generally accepted accounting alternatives.

2. Funds disbursed by the firm into the economy are included under "External Payments," and as such, this column is closely related to the usual funds flow statement. As a result of these payments, money is introduced into the economy to be respent with further contributions to GNP that may be far removed from any possibility of control or tracing from this firm's transactions.

3. Sulfur and particulate emissions are yearly aggregates based upon production and sales activity. The amounts attributable to productive activities are listed under "Total Manufacturing," while the emissions from "selling and administrative" activities are listed under that category and result from selling and distribution activities.

4. The economics of the sulfur removal program are displayed in the column, along with the resulting net loss.

5. The continued growth of the firm rests squarely upon the performance of 180,000 workers as displayed in the "Employment" column. Effective personnel policies have been the keynote of the firm, as output has increased at a rate significantly higher than that of inputs.

6. Intense efforts in the areas of health and safety are expected to result in a new low of only 218,000 lost workdays per year caused by accidents. Production time lost and accident classifications are projected to be consistent with OSHA standards of performance.

7. Integration of blacks and females into the organization is of utmost concern to top management. Overall black participation is well above average for the industry; however, in the area of female employment, present shortcomings are expected to change with an intensified recruitment program.

8. Semiskilled and unskilled labor are continually added to the firm's personnel roster. While on the job they receive training and instruction in manufacturing and administrative positions. Over 40 percent will leave the firm to accept employment elsewhere after their training period. Employment in this labor class is expected to be 2,000 for the coming year.

9. Corporate-owned housing is available to employees at reduced rental rates. There is an anticipated net change of 40 housing units next year; 75 blue-collar units will be done away with while 35 white-collar units will be added. A changing distribution of employment coupled with changing employee tastes is thought to justify this move.

Source: Claude S. Colantoni, W. W. Cooper, and H. J. Deitzer, "Budgeting Disclosure and Social Accounting," in *Corporate Social Accounting*, ed. Meinholf Dierkes and Raymond Bauer (New York: Praeger, 1973), pp. 376-77.

ple reemphasis in traditional financial information and a connecting of social performance data to usual categories, can be a useful step toward CSR. With the extensions of Table 6.5 profit impacts of various social programs are shown. Net income of this hypothetical company of $9.43 net of any environmental efforts is diminished to $6.40 with such activity. The profit impact associated with each activity would be helpful input in benefit/cost calculations to ascertain how scarce economic resources of a firm might be allocated. The data cited in this accounting elaboration is the cost part of the equation.

Table 6.6 on the same hypothetical firm shows alternatively that by rearranging usual data some useful insights can be reached. The external monetary impact of the company upon selected constituencies of employees, suppliers, stockholders, and government reveals something of the organization's economic importance. Hypothetical Occupational Safety and Health Administration (OSHA) index information can assist both managers and employees in ascertaining the distribution of costs to improve safety records. If, as the applicable footnote states, an index of 100 is taken to measure compliance with the act, then the per-ton cost data of Table 6.5 reflect the labor and capital costs required to bring safety levels, measured currently at 75, to full compliance. Performance evaluation is also facilitated by comparison over time of goals and results.

Finally, these documents indicate the necessity for narrative discussion to complement quantitative information for a more complete presentation. Numbers without descriptive background are indeed bare bones. Also, these extension proposals suggest that a simple choice between multiple and one-dimensional reporting need not be taken with CSR. Each category of social performance is presented in relevant measures, that is, pounds for pollution and participation ratios for black and female employment—and it is also translated into the single dimension of expenditures or cost per ton.

CONSTITUENCY FORMATS

A number of investigators have developed CSR systems based on disclosure as related to the interests of constituencies or various participants in corporations. James Shulman and Jeffery Gale have suggested such an organization;[7] Allan Shocker and Prakash Sethi have proposed an information system based on rather extensive attitude surveys, where performance criteria and priorities would be established to gauge the operations of major corporations.[8]

Undoubtedly the most well-developed and rigorous example of such a CSR structure is provided by the American Institute of CPA Committee on Social Me Measurement. They recognize as particularly relevant "publics" or constituencies the following: present and future generations affected by the environmental policies of enterprises; those, particularly consumers, influenced by business actions on nonrenewable resources; employees; suppliers; and local communities.[9] This investigation, a most comprehensive and exhaustive research effort, gives great detail concerning data and sources for each of the above categories.

Table 6.7 illustrates the considerable wealth of detail relevant to environmental concerns. The extensive material in Table 6.8 shows the kind of information applicable to employees and the sources of such material. These outlines are extraordinarily useful inventories of the topics of such disclosure for both internal and external purposes. Much of the data is available in company records, while other aspects require survey information and comparisons with other firms in the industry and community.

With regard to human resources, data is to be collected on income, security, and stability; physical work environment; psychological work environment; opportunity and equity; and an overall relationship category that takes into account such matters as grievances and complaints, work stoppages, alcoholism, and drug addiction. Obviously, the causal factors associated with these problems are more complex than simply the personnel practices of the employing corporation, but comparative studies may give clues about the strengths and weaknesses of particular companies' work setting.

One benefit of the AICPA study is its demonstration of how far research in disclosure on social performance has gone beyond earlier stages of vague, wishful thinking—to prescribing the contents of expanded corporate information systems. Increasingly, precise blueprints are available for detailed CSR. As noted in several instances, CSR is a valuable tool not only for external reporting but also for internal management purposes. Table 6.9 sets out a basic structure as proposed by the AICPA committee for a management-by-objectives evaluation of a particular corporate department or division. Corporate units are judged not only by budget and productivity performance but also by explicit goals relating to constituency expectations.

The AICPA structure or format has not as of now been put into full-scale use by any U.S. corporation. However, General Electric, a leading enterprise in the area of social measurement and policy, has operationalized at least one aspect of a constituency reporting system, that dealing with fair employment. It should be briefly scrutinized. As the materials indicate, GE has stepped beyond measurement to evaluation of divisions and their managers concerning employment goals for women and minorities. Their CSR system, an equal employment opportunity tool, is used primarily for internal management purposes.

This is not a program instituted only last year; they have audited internal performance regarding equal opportunity since 1970. Every general manager in the GE structure completes annually an extensive seven-page document that stipulates minority and female employment goals, five-year results and future estimates of performance, indexes of progress, detailed data summaries on employment at all levels, as well as thorough narrative statements describing programs, opportunities, and problems with minority recruitment, training, and promotion. Narrative documents also are collected on such matters as purchases from minor-

TABLE 6.7

The Environment: Suggested Information and Sources

General Area and Specific Attribute	Specific Information	Sources of Information or Evidence
Air quality		
Physical and chemical composition	Emissions of the five items included in ambient air quality standard; significant emissions of toxic materials	Measurements obtained by the use of measurement instruments, frequently carried out under procedures specified by governmental regulatory bodies; special technical studies
	Frequency and extent of violation of permitted levels	
Appearance (effect of color of smoke)	Frequency, intensity, and duration of unpleasant periods	Citizen perceptions; measurements using photographic and other methods of scaling
Odor	Frequency, intensity, and duration of unpleasant periods	Citizen surveys; intermittent observations and measurements
Water quality		
Physical and chemical composition	Discharges of metals, chemicals, pesticides, heat, radionuclides, oxygen dissolving and decomposing materials, microbiological contaminants and other effluents, particularly toxic effluents, affecting water quality	Measurements obtained by the use of measurement instruments, frequently carried out under procedures specified by governmental regulatory bodies; special comparisons with practical and available technologies
Appearance	Discharges affecting appearance, smell, and similar qualities	Intermittent observations and measurements; citizen perception surveys
Quality of use	Types of use (highest) permitted by quality of water	Special study
Noise and vibrations	Noise and vibrations noticeable outside facility	Intermittent tests; citizen perception surveys
Solid waste disposal	Quantities and waste disposal practices, including ultimate disposal of sludge	Special studies; internally developed quantitative data

Land		
Surface characterisitcs	Impact on terrain—on the quantity and quality of soil, erosion, water drainage, dust conditions, land cover, and the like	Engineering studies; studies of results of operating practices (as in farming and timber management)
Land use	Impact of types and amount of land use by facility on surrounding areas	Special studies
Ecology, flora, and fauna	Effects on the ability of an ecological area or system to support flora and fauna—with particular reference to diversity, endangered species, displacement of the more desirable by the less desirable, and the like	Special studies
Aesthetics		
Aesthetic quality of corporate facility as a free-standing unit	Attractiveness of exterior of building, grounds, and the like	Citizen perceptions; opinions of experts
Harmony, composition with surroundings	Suitability and attractiveness in terms of natural surroundings, other uses of land area, and the like	Citizen perceptions; opinions of experts

Note: The information that will be of most interest and value will be that which concerns the following:

1. Absolute quantities; comparisons with regulatory standards or known danger points; comparisons with performance in prior periods; relationship to best practical and/or available technology; comparison with others in the industry.
2. Share of total regional pollution.
3. Effects of major new facilities and activities (including construction).
4. "Irreversible" land uses.
5. Citizen perceptions and experts' views.
6. Corporate policies with respect to environmental matters and procedures.
7. Efforts made and planned to enhance the environment or reduce damaging effects; the results achieved or expected; capital costs; operating expenses, and cost recoveries.
8. Research and development efforts.

Source: Committee on Social Measurement, *The Measurement of Corporate Social Performance* (New York: American Institute of CPA, 1977), pp. 89-90. Copyright 1977 by the American Institute of Certified Public Accountants, Inc. Reprinted by permission.

TABLE 6.8

Human Resources: Suggested Information and Sources

General Area and Specific Attribute	Specific Information	Sources of Information or Evidence
Physical work environment		
Health and safety		
Severity and frequency of industrial accidents and illnesses (fatal and nonfatal)	Statistical information on frequency and severity, with identification of causes; additional information on good or bad situations	Internal records; OSHA reports, special studies, and analyses
Protection provided against exposure	Existing and increased efforts to provide protection against physical, chemical, and other risks attributable to materials, processes, equipment, and the like	Internal proposals, authorizations, departmental reports of safety programs, process changes, and the like, and analyses of results; results of OSHA audits and similar reviews by inside and outside experts
	Fatigue relief, and similar practices	Work practices; policy statements
Work place conditions		
Avoidance of essentially negative conditions	Situation with respect to such matters as work space (crowding); heat, light, ventilation; noise	Special studies and analyses;* comparisons with "good" practice as evidenced by government regulations, industry practice, and the like; surveys of employee perceptions and attitudes
Positive attractiveness	Aesthetics, cleanliness, and orderliness of plant, rest and restroom areas, food facilities, and the like	Special studies and analyses; surveys of employee attitudes and perceptions
Adequacy of resources to perform job	Adequacy of equipment, support facilities, organizational procedures and supervisory assistance to carry out work in time and manner expected	Surveys of workers and supervisors; special studies and analyses of indicated problem areas
Individual and public transportation (to and from the job)	Safety and availability of private and public transportation and parking	Surveys of employees; special studies and analyses

Psychological work environment		
Job content	Psychological satisfactions derived from work —current status, improvements, and the like Efforts made to increase work satisfaction through changes in work scope (usually via enlargement, greater challenges, and increases in responsibility), increases in variety, and the like	Special studies and analyses; surveys of employees
Coworker relationships	Positive aspects (e.g., cooperation, human interchange, and the like) Negative aspects (e.g., isolation, antagonism, tension, and the like)	Special studies and analyses; surveys of employees
Management-worker relationships	Basic management style —openness, communication, democracy/autocracy —tension and competition versus cooperation —work pace, handling of operational changes	Special studies and analyses; surveys of employees
Nonwork opportunities	Opportunities for personal and family leisure and recreation (vacation, holiday, out-of-town travel arrangements, and the like)	Policies and practices; surveys of employees
	Company-sponsored opportunities for employee participation in social, cultural, recreational activities as an extension of work relationships	Practices; survey of employees; data on participation
Personal assistance	Nature and extent of counseling on personal problems	Survey of employees; data on utilization
Opportunity and equity		
Employment distribution	Distribution of employment by groups, especially such disadvantaged groups as racial minorities, women, youth and aged, physically and mentally handicapped, the inadequately educated. Such information would include data on work	Personnel department records: EEO reports; comparable external data

(continued)

TABLE 6.8 *(continued)*

General Area and Specific Attribute	Specific Information	Sources of Information or Evidence
	force representation in total, by position classes, by stability of employment, and the like Efforts to improve distribution	Personnel policies and practices; data on activities and their effectiveness
Income, security, and stability Income Current income	Direct compensation (such as wages, salaries, commissions, bonuses, profit sharing) —in total —per capita compensation by deciles or quartiles —per capita compensation for meaningful classifications of employees	Payroll and personnel records
	—comparisons with industry and community averages (and with own data for prior years (and with changes in Consumer Price Index) —comparisons with U.S. government data on "income requirements," "poverty level cutoff," and the like, especially for lower deciles Fringe benefits of essentially short-term nature (e.g., health insurance)	Industry or community surveys, governmentally provided statistical data
Future income	Pension plans —essential elements —rights of employees, trusteeship, and the like —current cost, prior service liabilities —treatment of present retirees	Internal policy and practice statements, brochures Description of plans; corporate accounting and personnel records; survey of present retirees
	Social Security —current costs of corporate contributions	Accounting records

Income protection	Unemployment insurance payments to government and union plans	Accounting records
	Practices in terms of illness, long-term disability, death, and the like	Policies and practice statements
	Reemployment assistance	Policies and practice statements
Security and stability Overall situation	Statistical information as to —turnover and longevity of employment —involuntary turnover —days of employment per employee for year —reengagement/retention policies for whatever classifications of employees are most meaningful	Personnel records
Relationship to causes Schedule-related instability	Attribution of instability to major causes	Analysis of internal data
Obsolescence of skills and facilities	Nature, extent, and success of efforts to produce greater security and stability, including training efforts to prevent or compensate for technological obsolescence, transfer policies (relocations), peak/valley smoothing, and the like	Special studies,* policy/practice statements, analysis of training course content, and the like
Other, such as product discontinuance Uncontrollable variations, e.g., Supplier strike Customer demand Seasonability		
Employment opportunity facilitation	Actions to facilitate the employment of those with a personal disadvantage by such means as day care centers, special transportation arrangements, special prejob training and initial	Personnel practices; information on nature and extent of activities undertaken and employee utilization; survey of employees and of potential or former employees

(continued)

TABLE 6.8 *(continued)*

General Area and Specific Attribute	*Specific Information*	*Sources of Information or Evidence*
	orientation work rearrangements, and suitable hiring/testing/recruiting policies and practices; the results achieved	
Upward mobility	Actions to increase the promotability of employees, both directly on the job and by means of training opportunities, personality and health improvements; results achieved	Personnel policies and practices; activities undertaken as indicated by training and personnel department records; surveys of employees; personnel department records of upward mobility
Job creation	Increases and decreases in job opportunities through corporate growth or contraction—in total and by major position classes	Personnel department records
Overall		
Overall relationship	Evidences of company's overall relationship with its employees in relation to —voluntary resignations —absenteeism and tardiness —grievances and complaints —work stoppages —below-standard output —tension-related psychosomatic illness —alcoholism and drug addiction —suicides	Personnel department records; surveys of present and former employees

*It is assumed throughout that special studies and analyses would be made by insiders and/or outsiders with appropriate kinds and degrees of skill and appropriate degrees of independence.

Source: Committee on Social Measurement, *The Measurement of Corporate Social Performance* (New York: American Institute of CPA, 1977), pp. 115-19. Copyright 1977 by the American Institute of Certified Public Accountants, Inc. Reprinted with permission.

TABLE 6.9

Social Performance Status Report: Management by Objectives

Department————————————————Period————————————————

Departmental objectives

1. Financial

    Budgetary performance

    Productivity improvement of X percent

    Project A

    Project B

    Other efforts

2. Organizational

    Improvement of work environment

    Physical improvements

    Psychological improvements

    Minority and female employment

    Increase proportion of total to Z percent

    Increase proportion in executive positions to Y percent

    Safety

    Reduction in accidents and accident severity by X percent

    Special attention to process 3

    On-the-job and other employee training

3. Resource utilization

    Reduction in energy consumption by W percent

    Use of V percent recycled materials

    Reduction of quality-related rejects to U percent

4. Other

Source: Committee on Social Measurement, *The Measurement of Corporate Social Performance* (New York: American Institute of CPA, 1977), p. 214. Copyright 1977 by the American Institute of Certified Public Accountants, Inc. Reprinted with permission.

ity vendors and suppliers of the previous year and discussion of government reviews and complaints concerning equal opportunity.[10]

Judging from an analysis by Theodore V. Purcell, a careful student of the GE format, this corporation has linked EEO performance with executive compensation, though profitability, market share, and growth rate are clearly still prime considerations for promotion and pay improvement.[11] As might be expected, this kind of measurement/motivation tool has undoubtedly helped to increase markedly minority and female employment. As illustration of this, over the period 1968-73, GE experienced a 15 percent increase in total officials and managers; at the same time employment of women exploded by 297.5 percent and that of minorities by 247.7 percent. During the same period GE's total employees fell by 0.3 percent, while employment of women and minorities improved by 6.2 and 57.1 percent, respectively.[12] The GE experience strongly demonstrates that CSR used as a management vehicle can sharply improve business's social performance.

COMPARATIVE RATING FORMATS

So far there has been relatively little comparison between firms in a given industry or region with CSR. How well are we doing in contrast with competitors or companies whose plants are in the same region as ours? Interest groups can be counted on also to take a comparative look, to separate enterprises doing poorly relative to social expectations from those doing well or at least well enough.

A number of rating or comparison systems have been devised. For example, that described by Clair Sater was developed by a student group at the Stanford Business School. It involves a three-dimensional matrix looking at firms in an industry, areas of social concern, and comparison with other companies on a varied set of grounds including fulfillment of local legal requirements, and encouragement and cooperation with trade associations and government. Composite ratings are developed for each factor, which in turn has been weighted by significance. The companies in a given industry are thereby assigned social responsibility rankings.[13] R. D. Hay has also developed and experimentally applied a rating system[14] as has James M. Higgins.[15]

Perhaps the most noteworthy effort at comparing social performance within an industry has been that of the Council on Economic Priorities, a public interest research group involved in the area of social responsibility. In one case, after a careful examination of public and company data on pollution and pollution control expenditures, they, as a group of reasonably experienced—but outside and sometimes critical—observers, ranked the performance of selected corporations in the paper industry as good, average, or poor. Weyerhauser and Owen-Illinois received the highest ranking, while Potlatch, St. Regis, and Diamond were judged to have the poorest records in the industry.[16]

The primary advantage to incorporating ratings, rankings, and comparisons into CSR is that these ratings provide a basis when evaluation finally comes to look at relative performance—performance relative to goals or to what others are doing, and obviously it is difficult to judge performance in a vacuum. A serious disability of pure rating formats, however, is that inevitably subjectivity and opinion are involved in weighting the system's components and in grading the behavior of subject corporations. This criticism alone does not totally invalidate such devices; the studies, for example, do offer revealing indications of the diversity of behavior within a given industry. Evidence of this diversity makes it difficult to argue that all firms in an industry can hope to perform only at the lowest level. Nonetheless, subjective rating structures in CSR must be supported by a sound data base so that the evaluations can be deemed reasonable or rational.

PROGRAM MANAGEMENT FORMATS

Some researchers propose—and indeed some companies have already instituted— yet another type of CSR, a comparison system. However, instead of ranking the behavior of enterprises in an industry, this sytem compares performance with company goals for social programs. This format embraces a multidimensional view of CSR, for it is admittedly a one-shot look at company programs. No effort is made at finding a common monetary denominator on which to base a comprehensive evaluation.

The principal advocates of the social program approach are C. H. Brandon, J. P. Matoney, Jr., and Bernard Butcher of the Social Audit Research Group (SARG) at the University of Pittsburgh.[17]   The principal practitioners of this approach are the Bank of America and the SARG group at Pittsburgh. Program management in all these cases is goal-oriented, focusing on company objectives sought through a firm's specific social policies. Certain key questions are associated with this approach. "How well are we implementing these programs?" "What progress are we making toward achieving company goals?" "How effective is our effort at some kind of rough and ready benefit/cost analysis?"

Thus, program management looks at a tally of social programs' costs and benefits, though not in any fully quantitative sense. It monitors over time how the corporation is doing in terms of its social purposes. Table 6.10 gives an indication of how a program management document looks; Table 6.11 is another example. They are clearly management tools for evaluating performance. There is no effort to build an aggregate social balance sheet for the corporation. It is a tailored, focused look at specific programs, hence it is an easier initial assignment than developing an Abt-type balance sheet or income statement. To achieve the necessary understanding for the latter would require an extensive series of program management studies.

While it is primarily a company-based instrument for management, this type of program statement is surely undertaken with an awareness of social ex-

TABLE 6.10

Program Management Applied to a Bank Setting
(in thousands of dollars)

Minority Business Loans	1971	1972	Projected 1973
Cost			
Income			
Average loans outstanding	2,045	2,964	3,457
(x) gross yield (percent)	8.0	8.2	8.3
Interest income	163	243	287
Expenses			
Cost of funds	118	157	179
Making and servicing loans	20	18	32
Delinquency follow-up	5	6	10
Bank losses (90 percent guaranteed)	15	25	31
Total expenses	158	206	252
Net income	5	37	35
Opportunity cost			
Net return if funds had been invested at normal earnings rate	31	42	56
(−) net return-minority business loans	5	37	35
Total program cost	26	5	21

Benefits

Objective: To smooth the way for disadvantaged prospective entrepreneurs

About 25 percent of recipients would have qualified under normal loan criteria

30 percent have failed (one-half of whom blame the bank for the heavy debt burden or lack of follow-up counseling); 25 percent are marginal; 20 percent now operate successful businesses

Conclusion—Objective being met for some, but most disappointed

Objective: To increase minority employment opportunities

73 start-up businesses financed to date; 41 still in business employing 96 minorities and 37 whites

34 take-overs of existing businesses financed; 27 still in business; net increase in minority employment—23

Conclusion—119 new minority jobs created are important but insignificant compared to estimated 170,000 unemployed minorities (12 percent) in Detroit

Objective: To encourage capital inflow to minority areas

Most businesses small retail outfits; only four (total sales $510,000) sell goods or services outside minority community

Conclusion—Prime effect is slight reduction of capital outflow to extent that white businesses are taken over by minorities

Objective: To bring new business to MNB

83 percent of businesses still in operation use additional bank services

Profitability of added relationships estimated at $15,000 per year

Conclusion—Some small new business potential

Source: Bernard Butcher, "An Anatomy of Social Performance Report," *Business and Society Review*, Autumn 1973, p. 31. Reprinted by permission.

TABLE 6.11

Social Responsibility Program Statement

Program	Committed Resources	Effect on Human Behavior and/or Environment
Human resources		
Company medical plan	$——Health insurance contribution	——Number of employees covered ——Claims paid during year
Job safety program	$——Expended for noncompulsory safety equipment	——Injuries/1,000 man-hours
	——Man-hours spent on safety seminars and instruction	——Ratio of employee injuries to industry average
	——Suggestions adopted	
Leisure and recreation	$——	——Employees participants in softball league
	$——Land value	——Man-hour usage of company athletic facilities
Education	——Employees participating in company courses of instruction	——Employees successfully completing company courses of instruction
	$——Tuition paid	——Credit hours financed at colleges or universities
		——Degrees awarded to employee participants in tuition reimbursement program
Physical resources		
Company recycle program	——Man-hours spent on special studies	——Tonnage recycled ——Ratio of waste/final output ——Energy usage/final output
Land reclamation program	$——	——Ratio of reclaimed/damaged land
Product or service contributions		
Product safety	$——	——Product safety innovations implemented
	——Product research man-hours	
Packaging reduction	$——	——Reduction in tons of nonrecyclable packaging
	——Product research man-hours	——Tons of product or packaging recycled
Community involvement		
Local business development	$——Funds contributed	——Businessmen receiving free consulting
	$——Loans to minority	
	$——Business averaging	
	——Man-hours spent training unemployed	——Workers trained and removed from welfare
Community fund	$——Contributions	
	——Man-hours devoted to lecture on United Fund activities	——Percentage of employees contributing fair share

Source: C. H. Brandon and J. P. Matoney, Jr., "Social Responsibility Financial Statement," *Management Accounting*, November 1975, p. 33. Reprinted by permission.

pectations for business performance. Evaluations inevitably take place in a social context, thus reducing the possibility that the internal critique of business activity and the external critique by society-at-large will diverge, that company managers will set goals far removed from social requisites.

A "PROBABILISTIC FLOW" TECHNIQUE

The formats for reporting social performance examined thus far have had a "balance sheet" or "picture-at-a-moment-in-time" aspect, as have those methods characterized as social income statements. The latter are also static, "stock" depictions of an enterprise's social behavior. In contrast to these approaches, two Harvard analysts have developed a relatively simple yet quite valuable technique of studying the *process* or *flow* of change within an organization.

Neil C. Churchill and John K. Shank have devised a system for analyzing affirmative action progress with minorities and women based on the Markov-chain model of mathematics.[18] Using data on actual firms, transition probabilities can be calculated to reflect the likelihood of promotion of women versus men or minorities versus goals, for example. The objective of equal employment opportunity is a changed racial or sexual composition for a firm's management structure. The new mix and the rate at which it is achieved are both a function of the current pattern and hiring and promotion policies. The calculation of transition probabilities, such as those shown in Tables 6.12 and 6.13 for a particular milti-location retail enterprise, are a quantitative measure of promotion policies for men and women. The probabilities in the exhibit indicate the likelihood of being separated or promoted from any of eight job categories to any of the other positions. As illustration, in a given year women in position 4 had a .014 chance of advancement to position 6, while males had twice the chance of making such a jump, a probability of .028.

Reporting on social performance using this kind of format enables managers to come to some conclusions about upward mobility in their organizations. Are women on a different promotion track, faster or slower, than male employees? There was more jumping of promotion steps for men than women in this company, 61 versus 41. However, both matrixes are characterized by what Churchill and Shank call "diagonal drag," that is, the tendency to stay in the same job category from one year to the next. Promotion for either males or females was not a common occurrence.

This method of evaluating social performance can extend to a computer simulation of alternative hiring and promotion policies as they impact on a firm's management mix. It emphasizes the importance of transition probabilities—in everyday parlance, the promotion chances—in changing the character of a management team. Stealing top minority or female executives from another company is hardly what the social policy of equal opportunity visualizes.

TABLE 6.12

Transition Probabilities Matrix for Promotion of Male Employees, for a Selected Multilocation Retail Enterprise

Job Category at Beginning of Year	Job Category at the End of the Year								
	0	1	2	3	4	5	6	7	8
0	1.000	0.000	0.000	0.000	0.000	0.000	0.000	0.000	0.000
1	.200	.450	.200	.100	.050	.000	.000	.000	.000
2	.207	.010	.556	.101	.086	.040	.000	.000	.000
3	.115	.000	.033	.713	.102	.020	.012	.000	.004
4	.145	.000	.005	.023	.626	.150	.028	.023	.000
5	.140	.000	.014	.000	.021	.650	.091	.049	.035
6	.185	.000	.015	.000	.000	.031	.662	.092	.015
7	.147	.000	.000	.000	.000	.007	.042	.748	.056
8	.131	.000	.000	.000	.000	.000	.000	.024	.845

Source: Neil C. Churchill and John K. Shank, "Accounting for Affirmative Action Programs: A Stochastic Flow Approach," *The Accounting Review*, October 1975, p. 649. Reprinted by permission of the authors.

TABLE 6.13

Transition Probabilities Matrix for Promotion of Female Employees, for a Selected Multilocation Retail Enterprise

Job Category at Beginning of Year	Job Category at End of Year								
	0	1	2	3	4	5	6	7	8
0	1.000	0.000	0.000	0.000	0.000	0.000	0.000	0.000	0.000
1	.218	.595	.139	.044	.004	.000	.000	.000	.000
2	.152	.004	.750	.053	.024	.015	.000	.000	.000
3	.137	.000	.024	.742	.048	.048	.000	.000	.000
4	.113	.000	.028	.014	.676	.155	.014	.000	.000
5	.141	.000	.026	.000	.038	.692	.026	.051	.026
6	.000	.000	.000	.000	.000	.000	.786	.214	.000
7	.152	.000	.030	.000	.030	.000	.091	.667	.030
8	.009	.000	.000	.000	.000	.000	.000	.000	.091

Source: Neil C. Churchill and John K. Shank, "Accounting for Affirmative Action Programs: A Stochastic Flow Approach," *The Accounting Review*, October 1975, p. 649. Reprinted by permission of the authors.

Computer simulation, as illustrated in Table 6.14, makes it possible to ascertain whether given goals can be met through present policies. As the data indicates, a continuation of old promotion policies will not change the management mix. Even equal promotion rates, a kind of prima facie equity in policy, does not approach the company's publicly stated goals. (Given equal promotion rates, by 1985, 12 percent of senior management jobs would be held by minorities, and 13.8 percent by women, whereas the goals were 25 and 40 percent, respectively.) Such simulations are useful in appraising both the realism of corporate objectives and the effectiveness of policies. Churchill and Shank conclude from their study that equal opportunity should be defined in terms of hiring and promotion *rates* rather than a specific configuration of staffing. Affirmative action in terms of hiring and promotion will lead over time to definable percentages in all job categories.

This "probablistic flow" approach to CSR, concentrating on the *process* or movement of women and minorities up the management ladder, is a useful example of the potential for innovation in the evolving field of social disclosure. It holds promise as a complement to the more "stock" or "static" approaches to CSR. With discussion of this contribution to disclosure of social performance, the inventory of alternative formats is completed.

STANDARDS AND RECIPES FOR REPORTING ACTION

Research on CSR furnishes the alternative constructions and formats outlined here—and also stipulates a set of criteria or standards by which to evaluate the quality of such disclosure systems. The structure of standards illustrated in Figure 6.2, which is based on the analysis of Ralph Estes, is fairly clear. It rests on key requirements of relevance, freedom from bias, and cogency. Important but subsidiary to these key requisites are such factors as completeness, media propriety, and opportunity for rebuttal from constituency representatives.

The information must be in direct reference to the performance criteria specified by the American people and the participants in corporate enterprise, that is, it must be relevant to external expectations for U.S. business. Moreover, the data should not be so esoteric as to escape the comprehension of those using the reporting system. An additional criterion is the availability of information at local or regional levels as well as timely publication. The status of employee or product safety of five years ago does not meet the criteria of an effective information system. Independent attestation and the ability to verify the affirmations made by corporate management regarding social disclosure are also important. Finally, Estes recognizes the importance of comparison as a tool of evaluation and of quantification whenever possible.

With alternative formats and the standards by which to appraise their usefulness in hand, corporation managers interested in advancing the disclosure of

TABLE 6.14

Projections of Effects of Various Promotion Rates and Hiring Policies, for a Large U.S.-Based Financial Services Company

(percentages)

	Entry-Level Management		Middle-Level Management		Senior-Level Management	
	Women	*Minorities*	*Women*	*Minorities*	*Women*	*Minorities*
Present status						
1975	23.0	8.9	1.7	2.4	0.0	0.5
Publicly stated goals						
1980	32.9	15.0	14.9	12.2	10.1	12.2
1985	40.0	25.0	40.0	25.0	40.0	25.0
Plan 1: Affirmative action hiring: historical promotion rates						
1980	34.5	15.1	12.6	1.0	0.0	3.8
1985	44.5	19.2	24.9	1.0	0.0	5.8
Plan 2: Affirmative action hiring: equal promotion rates[a]						
1980	34.0	15.7	15.0	8.0	6.0	7.0
1985	41.0	20.0	25.6	15.0	13.8	12.0
Plan 3: Hiring only women: equal promotion rates[b]						
1985	75.4		42.2		22.1	

[a]These figures are based on historical rates for nonminority males.
[b]Minority representation is not considered in this particular run.

Source: Neil C. Churchill and John K. Shank, "Affirmative Action and Guilt-Edged Goals," *Harvard Business Review*, March-April 1976, p. 115. Copyright 1976 by the president and fellows of Harvard College; all rights reserved. Reprinted by permission.

FIGURE 6.2

Hierarchy of Social Reporting Standards

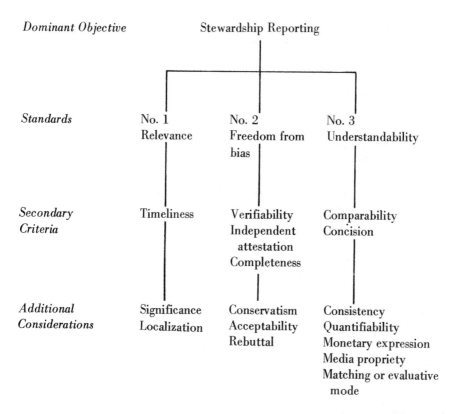

Source: Ralph Estes, *Corporate Social Accounting* (New York: Wiley Interscience, 1976), p. 156. Reprinted by permission.

social performance have several detailed "how-to" prescriptions for action. Frank Cassell, for example, outlines a six-step effort that includes an existing program inventory, analysis of current policies and corporate social objectives, evaluation of social program performance in the mode of Brandon and Matoney or Butcher, development of a goal-setting process with attention directed to short-range and longer-term policies and objectives, and, finally, communication with constituencies.[19]

Perhaps the most active CSR research group is that at the Harvard Business School organized under the leadership of Raymond Bauer, Robert Ackerman,

TABLE 6.15

Excerpt from the Harvard Management Process Audit Guide

Research Question: Has Corporate Policy Been Developed on the Social Issue?

Methodology
1. Obtain copies of policy statements, if any exist.
2. Interview personnel who drafted the statements.
3. Interview line managers to get their perceptions of the policy.
4. Interview CEO to get his views on the policy.

Procedural questions
1. What kind of analysis of the issue has the company made?
   a. Does the company know what the law requires? Or the relevant constituency expects?
   b. Has the company gathered information on how other companies in its industry handle the problem?
   c. Has the company inventoried its performance on the issue? What information has it gathered? If no audit has been performed, is one planned? Has it diagnosed its needs in social areas? Identified issues?
   d. Has the company researched what methods and tools are available to solve the problem?
   e. Has company identified the structural features and decision processes within the company that affect the implementation of policy on the specific issue?
2. In what form has policy been articulated?
   a. Has it been issued as a formal, written policy statement?
   b. Is it an informal memo?
   c. Was it issued verbally by the CEO?
   d. Is it unspoken, but still perceived and understood by most employees?
      [Questions 3 through 10 omitted]
11. If no goals exist, is the company in the process of setting goals?

Rationale

The formulation of corporate policy on a given issue may proceed by degrees and need not take place at any fixed point in the implementation process, though it ordinarily takes place at a rather early point. Statements of CEO commitment are usually too general to be much of a guide to action. A formal statement of policy is drawn up to be such a guide. While this is more likely to happen after a staff specialist has been appointed, it also may happen before that occurs. Since it may happen in either Stage 1 or Stage 2, the existence of a formal policy statement does not locate the organization firmly in either stage. While some organizations have renounced a formal policy setting even when at a fairly mature phase of Stage 2 on the grounds that it is not their style to have formal policies, we, with only some slight hesitation, conclude that a formal policy statement is a step forward in the implementation process—and probably a necessary one. If management of a particular firm believes otherwise, they should be pushed to defend that position.

A statement of policy ought to be based on and reflect an analysis of the substance of the issue and of ways of responding to it.

Almost all major social issues require the involvement of operating management. Hence, a policy statement that reflects the views and interests of line management is more likely to be effective and acceptable. On the whole, this is best done by involving them in the formulation of that policy.

We assume that the intent of the other procedural questions is self-evident.

Source: Raymond A. Bauer, L. Terry Canthorn, and Ronne P. Warner, "Auditing the Management Process for Social Performance," *Business and Society Review*, Fall 1975, p. 45. Reprinted by permission.

Neil Churchill. Their empirical work has been extensive enough to result in a practical manual for social auditing entitled *A Management Process Audit Guide*.[20] An excerpt from that manual is shown in Table 6.15. In it, a series of questions are used to guide the organization of an audit/disclosure system.

A detailed prescription has also been outlined by Terry McAdam, a management consultant with the McKinsey Company. He suggests as important ground rules early top management commitment to the project, performance appraisal with line management participation (a crucial point to be discussed later), and the establishment of modest initial social goals for the corporation. His outline for action includes identification of the performance categories to be studied, such as product line, employee relations, benefits, and work satisfaction; corporate philanthropy; environmental control; review of current performance across these activities; and analysis in depth of selected areas. Strategy should be developed for each area, with realistic goals set for revised and new programs. Finally, the programs should be implemented, monitored, and integrated into the basic management process. The organization assigned these tasks should include a social responsibility officer and department, particular task forces, and permanent board and management supervising committees.[21]

The AICPA research committee on social performance likewise recommends a number of procedural phases that include commitment of the organization, staffing, plans, and a detailed work program.[22] The content of a reporting system as stipulated by this committee, and as illustrated in Tables 6.7 and 6.8, frame an agenda for social disclosure. The staff's work program involves going to suggested data sources and "filling in the details." Clark Abt, moreover, furnishes precise timetables and organization specifications for the development of a "big picture" disclosure system. He estimates that a company on the scale of a *Fortune* 500 firm could expect the establishment and a first monitoring pass at the organization to require 45 person-months and a cost of $200,000-300,000, including full overheads.[23]

From this survey it is apparent that the current parameters of CSR encompass both an outline for an expanded corporate information net and procedures for development of more social disclosure. The next phase will be a strengthening of the preliminary work already under way in most large U.S. corporations. What lies ahead is indeed a formidable, though reasonably straightforward task, but at least the terrain has already been partly explored.

NOTES

1. Daniel Gray, "One Way to Go about Inventing Social Accounting," in Meinholf Dierkes and Raymond Bauer, *Corporate Social Accounting* (New York: Praeger, 1973).
2. Clark Abt, *The Social Audit for Management* (New York: Amacom, 1977).
3. David F. Linowes, *The Corporate Conscience* (New York: Hawthorne Books, 1974); and *Strategies for Survival* (New York: Amacom, 1973).

4. Ralph Estes, *Corporate Social Accounting* (New York: Wiley Interscience, 1976).

5. See "Auto Makers Play an Expensive New Game," *Business Week*, October 27, 1977, pp. 72-83.

6. Floyd A. Beams and Paul E. Fertig, "Pollution Control through Social Cost Conversion," *Journal of Accountancy*, November 1971, p. 37.

7. James Shulman and Jeffrey Gale, "Laying the Groundwork for Social Accounting," *Financial Executive*, March 1972, pp. 38-42.

8. Allan D. Shocker and S. Prakash Sethi, "An Approach to Incorporating Social Preferences in Developing Corporate Action Strategies," in S. Prakash Sethi, *The Unstable Ground: Corporate Social Policy in a Dynamic Society* (Los Angeles: Melville Publishing, 1974), pp. 67-80.

9. Committee on Social Measurement, *The Measurement of Corporate Social Performance* (New York: American Institute of CPA, 1977).

10. *Fair Employment Practices* (Washington, D.C.: Bureau of National Affairs), NO 183; 490, pp. 801-8.

11. Theodore V. Purcell, "How G.E. Measures Managers in Fair Employment," *Harvard Business Review*, November-December, 1974, pp. 99-104.

12. Ibid., p. 102.

13. Claire Sater, Committee for Corporate Responsibility—Corporate Rating Project, *Final Report* (Palo Alto, Calif.: Stanford Graduate School of Business, December 1971).

14. R. H. Hay, "Social Auditing: An Experimental Approach," *Academy of Management Journal*, December 1975, pp. 871-77.

15. James M. Higgins, "A Proposed Social Performance Evaluation System," *Atlanta Economic Review*, May-June 1977, pp. 4-9.

16. Leslie Allan, Eileen K. Kaufman, and Joanna Underwood, *Pollution in the Paper and Pulp Industry* (Cambridge, Mass.: MIT Press, 1972), pp. 44-45.

17. See David H. Blake and William Frederick, *Social Auditing* (New York: Praeger, 1977); C. H. Brandon and J. P. Matoney, Jr., "Social Responsibility Financial Statement," *Management Accounting*, November 1975, pp. 31-34; and Bernard Butcher, "An Anatomy of a Social Performance Report," *Business and Society Review*, Autumn 1973.

18. See Neil C. Churchill and John K. Shank, "Accounting for Affirmative Action Programs: A Stochastic Flow Approach," *The Accounting Review*, October 1975, pp. 643-56; and Neil C. Churchill and John K. Shank, "Affirmative Action and Quilt-Edged Goals," *Harvard Business Review*, March-April 1976, pp. 111-16.

19. Frank H. Cassell, "The Social Cost of Doing Business," *MSU Business Topics*, Autumn 1974, pp. 21-24.

20. Raymond Bauer and L. Terry Cauthorn, *A Management Process Audit Guide* (Boston: Harvard Business School, 1975).

21. Terry W. McAdam, "How to Put Corporate Responsibility into Practice," *Business and Society/Innovation*, Summer 1973, pp. 8-16.

22. Committee on Social Measurement, *The Measurement of Corporate Social Performance* (New York: American Institute of CPA, 1977), pp. 263-70.

23. Clark Abt, *The Social Audit for Management* (New York: Amacom, 1977), pp. 112-13.

7

AMBIGUITIES AND UNRESOLVED
SOCIAL DISCLOSURE ISSUES

The move to more sophisticated and advanced CSR systems, which use many of the proposals of the previous discussion as models, is facilitated by the valuable blueprints already at hand. In this respect the job is straightforward; however, a number of ambiguities, controversies, and unresolved issues confront managers interested in expanding social disclosure within their firms. Some of the issues may be false or are raised only because there is a premature call for choices of alternative reporting designs. A number of questions, nonetheless, present serious predicaments, which practitioners and researchers need to confront. An examination of the full range of issues, including both those that perplex and those that are sham, will help to further clarify CSR and its future.

COMPLEXITY OF DATA

One serious difficulty with CSR is that the facts of discrimination, product safety, employee relations, or pollution are generally influenced by complex, multivariate causal functions instead of simple, single cause and effect linkages. What is the conclusion to be drawn from a particular piece of social information, for example, that the employee turnover rate of a given enterprise is well above that of other companies in the same industry or region? Does it necessarily mean that the managers of that firm are derelict in their social responsibilities? High turnover rates may indeed be shaped by deplorable management practices—but also relevant here are the psychological characteristics of the work force, the state of the economy as it affects this particular enterprise, and choices made far back in the history of the company or region in which the corporation operates. Thus, simple conclusions from particular pieces of data may be thwarted by complex interplays of the many factors that have influenced a given company's behavior.

In addition, some elements of social disclosure may be difficult to evaluate as either "good" or "bad." Are high turnover rates due to dismissals and layoffs a sign of instability and poor human relations policies? Or are high quit rates an example of worker freedom in action as employees choose to move to better opportunities? The ambiguities and resulting tension from partly conflicting performance criteria and the existence of multiple causations for a given set of numbers all complicate the evaluation task.

Some data categories may lack the tension evoked by a mixture of desirable and undesirable elements, as may be the case with high employee turnover. It is difficult to muster a rationale for the conclusion that high employee accident and death rates on the job have some social good attached to them. But it is at the same time difficult to assess carefully the benefit/cost configuration associated with lowering employee injuries or deaths. In a world of scarce resources, what will be the full costs triggered by a given decrease in injuries?

This discussion has aimed at emphasizing the perplexities and complexities of evaluating the implications of what appear to be simple pieces of factual information. This state of affairs should not under any circumstances, however, force managers or investigators into a state of confusion and inaction. All other factors being constant, inquiry indicates high relative turnover rates are clearly a signal for deeper study. The messy assignment of penetrating to analyses and explanations of what is "really" going on is the unavoidable task of internal and external auditors of business social performance. There are few simple, mechanical connections between "the facts" and their causal base.

MEANS TRANSFORMED INTO REPORTING ENDS

Analysis is sometimes plagued with a tendency to shift attention from ends to means, displacing basic goals with a focus on the tools or means to achieve these objectives. This is particularly true in the case of CSR. As earlier discussion has noted, it is far easier to measure the inputs or means of corporate activity than it is the consequences embedded in the management process and a multifactor causal environment. Costs and outlays by a firm to combat the challenges of pollution, equal opportunity, and community welfare are easy to marshall into an explicit disclosure system. How much was spent last year in aid to education, reducing water pollution, or improving product safety? Simply look in the books for answers and report them in flowery displays of self-righteousness.

What is sought, however, are measurable improvements in output, better employment opportunities and safety, less water pollution, improved community welfare. These results of corporate activity are difficult to isolate and quantify. How much pollution improvement results from outlays by the XYZ corporation when it is interacting with hundreds of other sources of environmental degradation in a given industrial region? Reporting on business social performance can easily deteriorate to simple disclosure of expenditures and costs. The tough but significant job of elucidating the interaction of inputs and outputs in the "production function" of social performance is set aside for the simpler task.

American society primarily wants outputs or results, but it may find attention to goals displaced by a plethora of quantitative detail on the inputs of corporate expenditures. The link between social performance inputs and outputs may continue to be hidden in the relatively unexplored realm of causal interplay.

An example of the goal displacement "cop-out" in measurement and evaluation is seen in the area of health and medicine. Fundamental interest is directed to the complex objective of good health; but here, as with business social performance, the production function that specifies relationships between such factors as hospitals, medical personnel, and drugs and the output of good health is still plagued by confusion and ignorance. Hence statistics in the field are often directed to data on how many physicians and nurses are available per capita, how many hospital beds per 100,000 people serve a community, and annual expenditures on drugs and medical equipment. These are relatively easily measured inputs to the relatively poorly understood medical production function. You measure and report on the easiest pieces of the puzzle. It is simpler to ascertain how many doctors visits or hospital-days per year characterize different populations in the country than it is to explore why health differentials exist. Inputs rather than performance occupy center stage.

Perhaps it is reassuring in a backhand kind of way to see that transformation of means into ends with consequent measurement concentration on means is not limited to the field of CSR. It undoubtedly characterizes all complex processes about which there is considerable ignorance. Evaluation and measurement take the easy way out. But what goes on in some of these areas, such as the health field, is an arduous, slow job of building comprehension of the relationships between inputs and desired outcomes. With CSR, this kind of assignment can be a special priority of business schools and research institutes. Their relative impartiality, expertise, and interest in broad problems give them some research advantage. It is too large and general a problem for the interests of particular firms.

In summary, goal displacement is an obstacle to understanding in CSR as well as other complex areas. It should not serve as an excuse for inaction or shoddy efforts at disclosure of social performance.

DISCLOSURE OF VOLUNTARY VERSUS COMPELLED BUSINESS ACTIVITY

The disclosure of voluntary versus compelled business activity is an issue that arises from misunderstanding the nature of the social control of business behavior in contemporary society. David Linowes, an important scholar in CSR, is the principal advocate of the proposition that corporations should disclose in socioeconomic operating statements (SEOS) *only* those activities voluntarily instituted by the firm.[1] All activities and programs either required by law or labor contract or compelled by government agencies or labor unions would be excluded from such documents. It is disclosure only of voluntary, optional business practices presumably motivated by some altruistic interest.

Disagreement about this kind of allocation choice can be settled by recalling the nature of the interchange between business firms and the sociocultural system in which they operate. Corporate managers are instructed both by legislation and regulatory rule *and* by social expectations as to performance criteria and norms of business practice. Formal social control is supported and complemented by an informal set of norms and rules for coordinating business behavior. Sanctions in and out of the market help enforce these social requisites. Thus, it is erroneous to divide business behavior into voluntary and compelled. So-called voluntary decisions are shaped and directed by society's normative expectations. They do not spring spontaneously and uniquely from the imaginations and wills of corporate managers.

But to ponder questions of motivations and intent draws our analysis away from the fundamentals of social control. What is argued here is that the sociocultural conception of business motivation makes it all a social coordination process. Executives are schooled and directed in their "voluntary" activities just as society coordinates behavior through explicit law and court decisions. So in this context the distinction between voluntary and required is false. If requirements set by law are violated, then fines, bad publicity, and even jail sentences may result. If requirements outlined by norms and social expectations are violated, then sanctions of consumer agitation, employee turnover and deteriorating morale, or supplier court suits may be assessed. Programs prescribed by law or by norm are equally necessary costs of doing business.

Executives who really "believe" in what they are doing, genuine adherents to particular social objectives or norms, have been socialized to the degree that norms or requirements have been "internalized," to use the terminology of sociology. Policing of norms as part of an internal mental process is no less real than the employee resignations or threats of government legislation that keep expedient adherents in line. Thus, social accounting should cover all corporate activities that relate to social requisites, either in the guise of explicit regulation or in the form of normative definitions of behavior.

SHOULD CONSUMER SURPLUS BE COUNTED?

Both Clark Abt and Ralph Estes propose as part of their calculations of social benefits flowing from a firm that a "consumer surplus" component be included.[2] The sales of goods and services to customers reflect the fact that these commodities have value at least equivalent to the purchase price laid out for them. But these analysts argue further that in addition to the total sales of the company as a measure of social value, a consumer surplus should be calculated. Most buyers sense on occasion that if confronted with the necessity they would be willing to pay more for a product than the market price. The gap between the lower price actually paid and the maximum price consumers would be willing to pay is indication of a consumer "surplus." Abt and Estes did not discover the idea; it has long been a part of the literature of economics.

But a crucial question relates to the source of consumer surplus. If the source is the individual enterprise, then that surplus reasonably should be accounted for in totaling up social benefits of the firm. However, consumer surplus arises out of the dynamics of total market interplay, from macromarket forces rather than the behavior of individual, microunits in trade. The forces that push market prices down the consumer's demand curve, opening up the "surplus gap," are based in the facts of competition and technological innovation that expands supply. It is the large-number characteristic of most markets that push market price below consumer maximums. Furthermore, with competition firms cannot engage in discrimination, charging different prices for different blocks of product. It is a *single price* situation. The second factor at work in the total market or industry is technological innovation or advance in methods of production that increase supply and thereby push market price down.

Therefore, the source of consumer surplus cannot realistically be assigned to individual firms. Consumer surplus flows from forces at work in the total interplay of enterprises as they meet customers in the market. Chalk this benefit up to a *competitive market system* and technological advances that hit all firms in an industry. Consequently, the social benefits attached to individual companies should include only the sales value of goods and services produced for the market. CSR is a micro rather than an aggregate market-oriented measure of social benefits and costs.

CAN DOLLAR VALUES BE ASSIGNED TO CLEAN AIR OR HUMAN LIFE?

Economists, and perhaps calculating accountants as well, have a reputation for knowing the price of everything and the value of nothing! Here are individuals busily engaged in ascertaining the social costs of individual injuries and deaths when the view of many is that life is *beyond* measure. In addition, such investigators try to tally up the dollar value of clean air and water, when much of that value is intangible, psychological, and involved with subjective esthetics. A sunset on an ocean beach is something to enjoy rather than to pin down with dollars and cents.

As strong as they seem, though, these criticisms can be answered. First, a valuation process is unavoidable. Much of it is tacit and reflected in the daily decisions made by individuals or policy makers. In its hiring of police officers or deployment of ambulances a city is expressing what a human life or injury is worth in the community. A motorist recklessly speeding down the highway or a motorcyclist without a helmet is acting as though he has made calculations weighted without probabilities and based on estimates of what his or her life is worth. Property values where pristine waters flow and the air is invigorating and fresh reflect to some degree what social estimates are of these environmental goods. Thus, the valuation process goes on whether it is explicit or not. CSR is an effort to lay on the table avowed estimates of the impacts associated with the negative and positive social consequences of business behavior.

Second, the job of estimation is a formidable, difficult task. It does not pretend to encompass the full and compete social ramifications of business activity. Some costs and benefits cannot be readily quantified; they are intangible but nonetheless real. For example, in estimating the economic consequences of injury or death, few analysts attempt to put dollar values on psychological anguish, physical pain, and grief experienced by family and friends. What is tallied up, however, is an estimate of average social loss due to foregone production or income arising from premature death or disabling injury. Relatively simple techniques are available to make these calculations; these techniques, however, are open to criticism and improvement. A number of social scientists are engaged in strengthening the validity and accuracy of these approximation procedures.

Calculation of the social costs of industrial accidents or of pollution are reasonable efforts at getting at crucial pieces of data for enterprise and social decision making. Measures of the diminution of these costs are the "benefits" achieved through (corporate) expenditures on accident prevention and pollution control. They are clearly the lower bounds of the aggregate social costs of accidents or foul air and water; they are only *part* of the costs of negative externalities of business. They do not cover the waterfront, only key, measurable parts of it. The rationale for the practice is that often data on the lower limits of the total costs will be sufficient to indicate the right direction for personal, corporate, and social policy. The work is loaded with analytical snares and ambiguities, but clarification and increased understanding are expected payoffs from the effort.

CHOOSING UP SIDES

A survey of alternative formats and models for disclosure of social performance reveals a wide array of choices available to corporations. As has been seen, the diversity can be captured under the rubrics of "inventing," "stretching," or "incrementalizing," terms used by Daniel Gray but given different meanings here. Choices can be made between the analytical innovations of Estes' and Abt's "big

picture" approach and the extension of existing accounting documents as proposed by Beams and Fertig, Colantoni, Cooper and Dietzer.* Raymond Bauer and
Frederick Sturdivant call for the more pedestrian, simpler strategy of incrementally
building on accumulated data and procedures, foregoing global conceptions of
CSR.[3]

Another basis of choice rests in whether CSR should take the form of a
one-dimensional calculation in monetary terms, as Abt and Estes advocate, or
whether data should be disclosed in multidimensional terms congenial to the subject matter measured. Employee turnover, affirmative action programs, pollution
control, and corporate philanthropy, it is alleged, can be more readily addressed
in different definitions and units of account. A similar dichotomy exists in national "quality-of-life," the choice being between a Tobin and Nordhaus one-dimensional calculation of adjusted GNP as MEW (Measure of Economic Welfare) or
the multidimensional approach of the president's Office of Management and Budget.

This analytical "choosing up of sides" presents corporate managers with
what is in fact a kind of false issue. Some advocates argue that CSR should clearly
move in one of the possible directions enumerated here. Research and practice
should concentrate on a single choice, facilitating, it is contended, progress in the
field. It would seem, however, given the short life of CSR development, that it is
premature to focus resources and energies on a single approach.

With organized inquiry in CSR only about ten years old at best, the strategy
should be to let competition between alternate conceptions flourish with the hope
that in another ten years competition will more clearly indicate what are viable
approaches to social disclosure. The dilemma of choice can be postponed for a
time to enable a "survival of the fittest" evolution toward the best ways to go
with CSR.

THE PSEUDO EXTERNAL-INTERNAL CONFLICT

What is the purpose of CSR? Is it external stewardship evaluation or efficiency in the internal task of management? Is disclosure to constituencies and the
public-at-large the goal so that executives can be judged in their efforts at socially
responsible behavior? Or is CSR a management tool to improve the allocative task
of budgeting scarce resources to maximum payoff? As Ralph Estes argues, the
stewardship/usefulness contrast confronts traditional financial accounting as well
as CSR. These conflicting objectives or philosophies underlie the debate on a number of issues in traditional accounting, including that over historical versus current measures of costs.[4] Different conceptions of goals or purposes lead to basic
controversy in the field as a whole.

---

*See Chapter 6 of this volume on Types/Formats/Content and Procedures of CSR for
further discussion of these approaches.

One way out of the tension is to choose one goal as the primary purpose. Estes opts for this course with social accounting, selecting the stewardship function as the basic guideline. The aim of CSR is to assist all interested groups in evaluating the quantity and quality of social performance by business firms.

Another way to resolve the possible conflict between CSR as external stewardship evaluation and as an internal management tool for efficiency is to see them not in conflict but in some kind of logical ordering.. Social reporting can be viewed as an integral element in the informal social control of business behavior. Given the varied yardsticks for behavior prescribed both by society and corporate constituencies a widened information system is essential for behavior appraisal. Thus, the prime purpose of CSR is social monitoring, emphasizing the necessity for balanced, accurate disclosure about corporate performance.

However, given this fundamental purpose, executives as managers of corporate organizations need similar documents to aid them in coordinating business actions toward fulfillment of varied community purposes. Given the broad goal of evaluating managerial stewardship in the administration of society's purposes, subsidiary tools and devices are required. Internal social reports are instruments by which managers carry out the intraorganizational challenges of meeting social and constituency goals. To do their job, managements require information on gaps between behavior and purpose and data about subunit performance, not only financially but socially.

It is not an either/or choice between social reporting as external or internal instruments. The necessity for disclosure to the community-at-large triggers in turn administrative requirements of internal documents for monitoring, budgeting, and motivating the corporation's work force. Sharply managed enterprises will carry out both external and internal monitoring processes, that is a widened corporation information net will have both external *and* internal facets.

One example of information that could be developed in both internal and external documents is found in the joint research of an accountant scholar and a public accounting executive. Michael Alexander and J. Leslie Livingstone organized a benefit/cost study for a large utility company on the impacts of air pollution. The conclusion that the benefits of control through diminished pollution greatly outweigh the costs of control are valuable both to external groups of citizens, environmentalists, and regulators—and to executives grappling with capital expenditure policies. Had the data supported the opposite conclusion it would have been equally valuable to external groups and to utility management.[5]

PURE RATIONALITY VERSUS "MUDDLING THROUGH"

An issue of marked importance for CSR arises from the debate over the nature of the public policy process in the United States. Indeed, the nature, meaning, or intrinsic character of CSR is a direct result of that debate. According to some observers, public policy formation is essentially a rational procedure built on the style of individual decision making. According to that conception, initial agreement on goals is followed by a rough but discernible weighing of the pros and cons of alternative means of action and then the application of the selected alternatives to those goals. Logically and realistically ends come first, followed by a careful, explicit evaluation of the relative strengths of means to achieve given ends. This is the conception of elementary microeconomics.

CSR becomes a key element in such a rational model, for presumably social choices are best made with disclosure about the pros and cons of various approaches to consensus ends. Admittedly, it is possible to have too much information when all the costs and benefits are toted up. But, on the opposite side, choices between alternatives in the face of accepted criteria are facilitated by knowing something about results of social goals. Optimum choices are more likely given knowledge about the benefit/cost configurations associated with various means to achieving particular goals. As is apparent, the philosophy of this general examination of CSR has been built on the order of this rational model. The accounting approach to disclosure, likewise, is constructed in a rationality mode. Goals exist, corporations behave, and it is useful to know something about particular means-ends juxtapositions.

There is, however, an opposite view of the U.S. public policy process that raises questions about the basic character of CSR. This "muddling through" conception posits that ends and means are *simultaneously* explored and defined in a heavily "political" interplay. Performance criteria rise and fall in prominence as they strike the emotions and minds of the American people. Attention is directed to one goal and then to another as events and pressures influence the process.

The public policy interchange itself helps to clarify the meaning and content of goals. Performance criteria are not thrust into the fray pure and undefiled from some exterior source. They are defined and developed in the crucible of public policy debate as means are considered and consensus is sought. Debate about social security, wage and price controls, affirmative action and reverse discrimination, antitrust and economies of scale, pollution, and the energy crisis assists in an evolving understanding of the purposes and goals of the U.S. economy.

"Politics," not rationality, is the primary motivation for decision in this conception. Here, criteria or ends are more fluid than the rationality perspective supposes. Conflict between interest groups in defining means and ends is a main feature of the process.

With this conception, CSR is not so much an *instrument* of rational decision making as a *weapon* in the hands of warring parties as they seek particular inputs into public policy. Environmentalists and civil rights activists will manipulate data for their goals just as executives will seek to put the best interpretation on the social performance of business.

The second model gives at least partial insight into the nature of political truth. If that is the case, then varied participants, including business, in the democratic maelstrom have little choice in whether or not they engage in CSR. Advocates on opposite sides of issues can be counted on to use data merely as a debating tool to influence opinion. With this vision of the democratic policy process, rarely would CSR be a pristine, neutral, and objective adjunct to rational decision making. It is an integral aspect of political campaigns to shape America and its future. Here social responsibility has the overtones of an ideological weapon in the political struggles to control the character of the economy.

VOLUNTARY OR COMPULSORY DISCLOSURE OF SOCIAL PERFORMANCE

Controversy rages over whether CSR should be the voluntary choice of corporate managers or another government requirement within which a business system functions. A considerable amount of financial disclosure is already provided by law for investors, under a kind of "consumer protection" motif. Investors can be viewed as purchasers of securities who for purposes of fairness and efficiency require a great deal of financial data in order to make intelligent buying decisions. The question is whether the disclosure principle should be extended by the SEC or Congress to include the interests of other corporate constituents and the general citizenry.

It is a difficult issue to resolve; controversy about the matter very probably will increase in the future. Some aspects of the question, however, can be set out, perhaps clarifying the issue in modest ways. First, present levels of CSR cannot be considered fully "voluntary." To be sure, legislation does not provide for CSR, nor does the SEC require social disclosure beyond minimal amounts as social matters bear materially upon corporate financial health. Nonetheless, given social expectations and pressures by participants in companies, it seems inescapable that some social disclosures will be made, certainly by large corporations. This apparently is the conclusion of about 85 percent of the *Fortune* 500 largest industrial corporations. This is the proportion of those firms that presently engages in some degree of social reporting. Thus, the choice is not between voluntary and required CSR, but between an informally encouraged, mandated system and a federally sponsored structure of social disclosure.

Second, to the degree that public policy on many issues important to business is framed in a complex interplay of political dialogue, controversy, and concession, some kind of social reporting would appear to be a wise and sophisticated move by corporate managers. It is what some observers have called a "proactive" strategy, one anticipating pressures and softening their impact by cooperation and compromise. Such a maneuver of sophisticated "voluntarism," however, may have a deficiency. From the perspective of rational evaluation of corporate and social alternatives such CSR activity may be insufficiently objective and balanced to make possible reasonable choices.

Some would argue that only the excessively naive would expect corporate managers to be supersophisticated in the public policy debate and devise fully balanced, authoritative systems of social accounting. The fear is that if the purpose is political or ideological, the results will be selective and aimed at persuasion rather than realistic measurement.

However, to indicate that policy formulation is complex—and involves many players—corporate managers even in the absence of disclosure legislation increasingly receive instructions from many sources about the construction of reporting systems. Professional accountants and their organizations, university scholars, research institutes, and consulting firms make impossible a unilateral design for social disclosure. As this study reflects, these players propose formats and content for social reporting, and leading corporations show by example what real-life reporting systems look like.

Third, it is useful to recall the rationale for government stipulation of a widened corporate information system that is virtually explicit in this study. Building on the arguments of Christopher D. Stone,[6] a reasonably balanced and objective structure of social disclosure, and companion organizational changes within the large corporation, may be set forth as trade-offs for detailed government intervention. Stone builds an impressive case for the position that government regulation presently is a deficient control mechanism for fostering the public interest. If self-policing were given rigor and substance, with corporate decisions in the full glare of publicity and disclosure, it can at least be argued that other government intrusions as a quid pro quo could be diminished. Some advocates for a genuine CSR see it as a way of building support for a contemporary market system. Required social disclosure thus need not be interpreted as simply another incursion of government into the private domain. It may be the means for a *net* rollback of government participation in the economy.

Finally, how each individual responds to the question of voluntary versus compulsory disclosure rests partly on how sturdy informal social control appears to be in contemporary business. If norms and social yardsticks are seen to have some prescriptive substance, then the necessity of government specification diminishes correspondingly. On the other hand, if serious disbelief exists in social ordering through norm and expectation, then the case is stronger for government enforcement.

NOTES

1. David F. Linowes, *Strategies for Survival* (New York: Amacom, 1973), chap. 11; and *The Corporate Conscience* (New York: Hawthorn Books, 1974).

2. See Clark Abt, *The Social Audit for Management* (New York: Amacon, 1977), pp. 23-27, 183; and Ralph Estes, *Corporate Social Accounting* (New York: Wiley-Interscience, 1976), chap. 5.

3. Raymond A. Bauer and Dan H. Fenn, Jr., *The Corporate Social Audit* (New York: Russell Sage Foundation, 1972); and Frederick Sturdivant, *Business and Society: A Managerial Approach* (Homewood, Ill.: Richard D. Irwin, 1977), chap. 19.

4. Ralph Estes, "Standards for Corporate Social Reporting," *Management Accounting*, November 1976, pp. 20-21.

5. Michael O. Alexander and J. Leslie Livingstone, "What Are the Real Costs and Benefits of Producing 'Clean' Electric Power?" *Public Utilities Fortnightly*, August 30, 1973, pp. 15-19.

6. See Christopher D. Stone, *Where the Law Ends: The Social Control of Corporate Behavior* (New York: Harper Colophon Books, 1975).

8

THE ORGANIZATIONAL POLITICS
OF SOCIAL REPORTING

Politics can be viewed as a key ingredient in the business-society inter-change, in the wrestling within pluralistic democracy to frame goals and to com-prehend the impact of alternative approaches to these goals. But political ferment is also a vital dimension in the institution of social responsibility *within* large cor-porate organizations. So far this discussion of CSR has concentrated on essentially technical aspects of social disclosure, exploring its history, rationales, and formats.

There are, however, other components to social responsibility and the re-lated matter of disclosure of corporate performance. The environment of CSR is that of large business enterprises, exceedingly complex human organizations. For social responsibility and CSR to move beyond glib generalities in scholarly jour-nals and executive speeches requires formidable *intra*organizational tasks of *man-aging* social responsiveness and disclosure. There are psychological and political challenges with this assignment that present serious pitfalls to an institution of social disclosure systems. Such systems will not spring full-blown from top exec-utives' broad policy pronouncements.

To be sure, the task today is probably easier than it was a decade ago, since executives recruited to business increasingly have grown up with widened awareness of the social issues facing business. U.S. business schools now have curricula and programs aimed at informing and sensitizing graduates who in the future will occupy powerful positions within large corporations. The external en-vironment and the recruits to business management have both changed. Nonethe-less, given present corporate structures and incentive systems, the managerial chal-lenge for CSR is a serious one.

Frederick Sturdivant, a senior scholar in business and society, has outlined a number of organizational barriers to managing social responsiveness within cor-

porate enterprise.[1] First, corporations are indeed built on the style of the Carnegie-Mellon organization theory model of behavior. Large firms do tend to respond
to social issues and problems in a crisis, fire-engine manner, moving as difficulties
arise, but forgetting about them as the immediacy of the challenge fades. Other
deficiencies and shortcomings arise to pull their attention in other directions; so
policy making and action tends to be ad hoc and temporary. Long-range plans
and permanent organization are not built to meet the onslaught of social issues.

Second, too many enterprises respond to crises and controversy in a public
relations way that accentuates the positive and seeks to convince and persuade
the community that the firm is indeed socially responsible. This response philosophy is hardly the proper setting for the establishment of a sophisticated social
reporting system. Slogans and incomplete presentations rather than candid disclosure characterize this type of managerial effort. Rather than being convinced
of the validity of business policies regarding society, corporate constituencies become cynical, tough advocates for even more radical change.

Another serious handicap to the development of balanced, objective social
disclosure, as Sturdivant argues, is the strong trade-secret mentality on the part
of many executives. Even in the United States, where disclosure of corporate information is far more thoroughgoing than in any other nation, too many managers take the view that "it is nobody's business" what is done within the confines
of corporate enterprise. Factual data reported by law to federal agencies in the
areas of pollution, safety, and fair employment are nonetheless withheld from
wider public distribution. Fear of competitive disadvantage and adverse publicity
and of possible court suits and too often an adversary attitude generates the
strategy of minimal presentation of social data and description. In counterpoint
to a corporate secrecy policy are strong public and constituency pressures for
more social and financial disclosure. A foot-dragging, negative approach to disclosure is likely to backfire in even more expanded dissemination of information
given the present social and political climate.

The fourth barrier, very probably the most burdensome one, is based in organizational inertia and disinterest accentuated by measurement and incentive
systems that concentrate on financial performance. CSR expressly is part of a
widening of business objectives or constraints to include more than profits,
growth in sales, or market share. Yet existing monitoring and compensation procedures in most enterprises underscore and concentrate on these latter goals. To
complicate the decision-making responsibilities of executives with widened goal
and constraint sets hardly evokes their support and enthusiasm. Individually they
may applaud the idea of a more socially sensitive enterprise, but institutional
pressures and requirements push them toward concentration on financial performance. It is almost universally asserted that business life is complicated enough
as it is.

Fortunately, however, recent research has been completed by Robert W.
Ackerman, whose credentials include both top management experience and aca-

demic scholarship at Harvard, which greatly assists in understanding these organizational challenges. His research, furthermore, offers a recipe for institutional innovation fostering greater social responsiveness in business. He dissects the problem and in the process illuminates the path toward successful management of social responsibility.[2]

The Ackerman work is founded on a number of field studies investigating the complexities of responsibility in the organizational context of large corporations. It is not armchair theorizing, but the development of frameworks based in inductive research. The first insight is an emphasis upon the administrative dilemmas generated by the divisional form of corporate structure. Except for their basic performance requisites and guidelines divisional managers are largely independent decision makers, running their "shops" as they see fit.

One of the fundamentals of any complex organization is that rarely can the chief executive issue orders, and expect administrators to respond instantaneously, leaping in unison. Top managers are powerful persons, to be sure, but the inertia, rigidities, communication gaps, and independence of middle managers insulate them from topside orders to a considerable degree. Presidents of the United States, governors of the largest states, and corporate executives have all learned this sobering lesson. It is particularly the case with divisionally organized enterprises. Chief executives cannot bring policy changes to pass by fiat—and this clearly applies with regard to social concerns of business.

Ackerman also recognizes that the institution of social policies and procedures such as CSR involve time and a particular kind of *process*. The process of moving from initial interest to policy in place along with institutional structures and monitoring is succinctly summarized in Table 8.1. The Ackerman research leads to the conclusion that this depiction is the typical sequence of activities as social responsibility is operationalized within business. The whole continuum of events extends over a period of time, perhaps six to eight years, so patience is one virtue recommended for those interested in seeing a solidification of social performance.

The first phase is taken up with chief executives shaping and strengthening broad commitments toward more social action. This is done by a variety of communication efforts and modest adjustments of budget priorities, setting the stage for genuine achievements. The process could stall here, for the energies and attention of chief executives can easily be drawn to other important issues facing the firm. Furthermore, as earlier noted, general pronouncements from the chief executive's office may evoke expressions of approval, but they alone are insufficient to generate the organizational specifities that bring social responsibility alive.

The formulation of policy by the CEO is nevertheless a necessary preliminary to further development. One lesson from experience seems to be that if the top officer does not strongly advocate a responsibility action stance spread through the organization very little will come to pass. His support and clarification of purpose leading to increased awareness that social policies have high priority is fundamental in the initial phase of the total process.

TABLE 8.1

Conversion of Social Performance from Policy to Action

Organizational Level		Phases of Organizational Involvement		
		Phase 1	*Phase 2*	*Phase 3*
Chief executive	Issue:	Policy problem	Obtain knowledge	Obtain organizational commitment
	Action:	Write and communicate policy	Add staff specialists	Change performance expectations
	Outcome:	Enriched purpose, increased awareness		
Staff specialists	Issue:		Technical problem	Provoke response from operating units
	Action:		Design data system and interpret environment	Apply data system to performance measurement
	Outcome:		Technical and administrative learning	
Division management	Issue:			Management problem
	Action:			Commit resources and modify procedures
	Outcome:			Increased responsiveness

Note: Phase 1—social concerns exist but are not specifically directed at the corporation; *Phase 2*—broad implications for the corporation become clear but enforcement is weak or even nonexistent; *Phase 3*—expectations for corporate action become more specific and sanctions (governmental or otherwise) become plausible threats.

Source: Robert Ackerman and Raymond Bauer, *Corporate Social Responsiveness: The Modern Dilemma* (Reston, Va.: Reston Publishing, 1976), p. 128. Reprinted by permission.

The broad sequence of events leading all the way from policy to behavior is that of policy, learning, and, finally, organizational commitment. To introduce new criteria, standard operating procedures, and a widened outlook involves institutional innovation of a most significant order. Thus, a considerable body of technical and human relations expertise must be assembled to facilitate such an innovational accomplishment.

As Figure 8.1 shows, this process requires the employment of corporate staff specialists whose tasks are manifold. These staff personnel are variously titled as vice-president of social affairs, or of public affairs, vice-president for community relations, or manager of environmental affairs. Many, as these titles indicate, have vice-president status. They and their newly organized departments must be sensitive scanners of the business environment, collecting and analyzing information about issues on the business scene. In addition, they are organizational catalysts who in tactful, careful ways focus the corporation's attention on the particulars of relevant controversies.

They are facilitating experts whose ultimate purpose is to assist divisional officers in the development of new information systems, new priorities, and monitoring operations for the firms. Without these energizing executives the management of social responsibility would be left at the level of vague good intentions. Figure 8.1 demonstrates aptly the "person in the middle" characteristic of social-issues staff specialists. Tension, challenge, ambiguity, and uncertainty inevitably pervade their work experience. The intricate web of relationships that flow through staff specialists involve encounters that can easily deteriorate into distrust and suspicion.

The president may wonder whether the "issues" vice-president is sufficiently loyal, fearing "sell-out" to complaining interest groups. From the point of view of social agencies, the specialist is a "company person" likely to give the corporate establishment view on everything. They may see him or her as a sophisticated manipulator of enterprise public relations. At the same time, social agencies are important sources of information and dialogue for the staff expert. Division managers, on the other hand, can easily conceive of the specialist vice-president as an ivory tower, do-gooder outsider who has forgotten the financial fundamentals of the corporation. Yet line officers receive vital assistance from social affairs officers as they are pressed in the direction of making real corporate commitments toward social action.

Each of these interacting groups greatly need the broker role exercised by ranking specialist executives. This person and department are the social-agency interface with the company, an organizational unit that should be counted on to be sensitive to their demands. Division managers left without specialist knowledge and encouragement cannot effectively participate in shaping the new priorities and control systems that will be elements in their decision-making environment. Regulatory agencies will end up doing the designing and defining.

It is no wonder given these extraordinarily charged interplays that many observers have stipulated that officers in social issues must be patient, knowledge-

FIGURE 8.1

Relationships in the Social Response Process

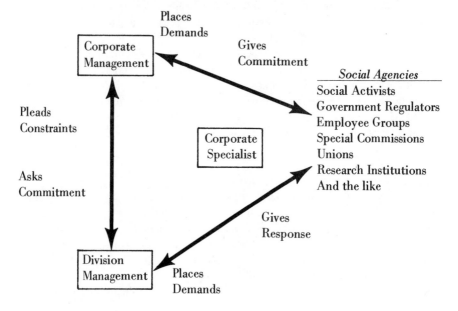

Source: Robert W. Ackerman and Raymond Bauer, *Corporate Social Responsiveness: The Modern Dilemma* (Reston, Va.: Reston Publishing, 1976), p. 323. Reprinted by permission.

able politicians, negotiators, and mediators. Their main weapons generally are expertise and educational persuasion rather than organizational power. Strong support by the chief corporate officers is essential, but their success is achieved primarily through astutely negotiating and compromising to create new policies and procedures for the enterprise. Their work assignment, absolutely essential for success in managing social responsiveness, includes designing, in cooperation with headquarters and divisional executives, the institutional innovations that transform noble thoughts into specific corporate behavior. Expanded corporate social reporting systems are key elements in their stock in trade involved in building a broadened corporate monitoring and control apparatus.

As Table 8.1 indicates, the final phase of making operational organizational commitment to broadened corporate purposes involves the participation of all principal elements in the administrative structure. But, first, what are the specificities of such organizational commitment? As has been apparent throughout the discussion, broadened corporate purposes refers to the easily stated but not so easily achieved enrichment of the enterprise information or accounting system and its monitoring procedures to encompass social performance. It includes re-shaping executive compensation systems to put salary and bonuses in line with the enlarged goals of the corporation. CSR is a key piece of this organizational innovation, the elaboration of information documents of the firms, and conse-quently in its internal dimension an inherent aspect of performance monitor-ing procedures.

Chief corporate officers, social issues specialists, and division managers are in a real sense partners in the enterprise of developing these management processes. Top management and division officials in a participative interchange frame the particular performance criteria for the company and, with staff spe-cialists in a consultive capacity, jointly shape the enlarged management vehi-cles of control. Given these changes, social responsibility may come more alive as an integral part of marketing, manufacturing, capital expenditure, and person-nel decisions.

This genuinely political process of evolving new corporate procedures and institutions is guaranteed to be full of difficulty, controversy, and organizational trauma. But Ackerman concludes from his field studies of U.S. companies work-ing through such transformations that there is potential for "creative use of trauma."[3] Out of the ferment may come the development of corporations bet-ter able to meet the varied social expectations that the American people in all their diversity place on the agenda of contemporary business enterprise.

NOTES

1. Frederick Sturdivant, *Business and Society* (Homewood, Ill.: Richard D. Irwin, 1977), pp. 114-16.
2. Robert W. Ackerman, *The Social Challenge to Business* (Cambridge, Mass.: Har-vard University Press, 1976).
3. Ibid., p. 126.

9

FUTURE PROSPECTS
AND IMPLICATIONS

After this detailed exploration of CSR, an inquiry into its relationship with corporate social responsibility, its rationales, history, structures, issues, and politics, the subject has been laid bare and dissected. Clearly, no executive should now plead ignorance or confusion about the nature of CSR. Specificities of format, content, and procedure for instituting a social disclosure system proliferate from the work of professional experts. Committees of accountants in several professional bodies and many others have made significant contributions in charting the future course of CSR.

Counterbalancing this conclusion of growing knowledge is the advice of feigned ignorance that research should be encouraged on all fronts. At this stage no particular approach to social disclosure can be seen to have outrun its alternatives. The strategy now should follow the famous early Maoist counsel, "Let a thousand flowers flourish."

At this point CSR is largely a "market" kind of expansion of existing accounting systems. To be sure it is a development in a context of government legislation concerning such matters as pollution, fair employment, consumerism, and employee safety. But disclosures in place at the moment have been evoked by a wide set of demands and pressures on business. It is a part of informal social control—presently informal and evoked rather than compulsory, as with disclosure of financial data. This does not mean to say that a required CSR is necessarily off-limits, but simply that thus far it has been a response of U.S. business to have felt pressures from such elements as the accounting profession, corporate constituents, and concerned observers. It is in the market pattern of demand generating a supply.

The future pace of advance is somewhat uncertain. Clearly, it will be a long-term, unfolding course of action, even though considerable work has already been done. The pace will be influenced by whether the demand of investors for more social data accelerates, encouraging the SEC to require more such information, whether the accounting profession strongly advocates a widened reporting and auditing of business activities. Finally, it is influenced by whether Congress provides for compulsory disclosure. It seems likely, however, that present momentum toward more social reporting will continue in any event. The pattern may be uneven, one of fits and starts, explosions and plateaus. This is the usual scenario with most innovations, and it could be expected to be the pattern with CSR.

It is clear that the present circumstance of CSR is not one of "market saturation." More intensive and deeper reporting is the expected long-run trend. If the process is examined while it is in a plateau or doldrums stage, it is easy to be pessimistic about the future. At the same time, if one focuses only on a period of accelerated expansion, it is equally easy to be excessively optimistic about the pace of development.

In any case, it will happen piecemeal and incrementally, slowly drifting in like the fog rather than with a sudden clash of cymbals a la the public announcements of personnel and policy changes in the Peoples Republic of China. It will come not in a rush but one step at a time, with joint decision and exploration about content and format. Accounting professionals will have more to say in the future about design and process with social disclosure. No company will be able to "go it alone" in a growing participative CSR environment.

Turning now to the social significance of CSR, it is part of a modest transformation of economic institutions in the United States. The transformation on a scale of change is at the level of adjustment rather than revolution. It is a double-faceted institutional change in the sense that intrafirm practices undergo a certain metamorphosis that, in turn, has ramifications for the functioning of a market economy. With it a market economy takes a moderate parametric shift toward greater attention to an enlarged set of socioeconomic performance criteria.

The life of the business manager, however, is undoubtedly complicated by these micro/macro institutional changes. It is laced with more complexity and ambiguity than a simple short-term profit conception comprehends. Recruitment of individuals to fill these difficult positions, however, seems not to suffer. In fact, the enriched and expanded elaborations of business behavior described in this study may make it easier to secure capable executives, given the philosophy and values of many youthful Americans. The hard-nosed, profits first, last, and always stereotype of business fades with the necessity for responsive, sensitive, coping managers in the modern world.

In this evolving setting, business firms hardly lose their fundamental social role of "turning out the groceries," nor are profits dismissed as unnecessary.

But profits are sought and production generated within a context that recognizes that other social and constituency demands are also important. This changing environment, however, does underscore the cruciality of corresponding elaborations on traditional business education to enable new volunteers to management to better cope with complexity and ambiguity.

Finally, it is institutional change in the best reformist American tradition, where dialogue, participation, goodwill, and reasonable intelligence are charting the course. The work focused around CSR is a detailed exploration of pros and cons with little expectation of optimal change, something unexciting compared to the grand ideological battles of the left and right. These latter loud exchanges, however, rarely exert significant leverage upon the nation's socioeconomic perplexities. A reasoned dialogue about the stance and content of contemporary capitalism holds more promise for meeting these issues and within the context of a free, market economy.

It is reformist and both liberal and conservative. Its aim is saving capitalism from an excessively narrow emphasis that may provoke more radical change. Daniel Moynihan has drawn attention to the fundamental problem. His diagnosis is that "the difficulty is simply that a mind attuned to the market place acquires an almost trained insensitivity to nonmarket considerations."[1] The goal of CSR in a market system is to counteract such trained insensitivity with widened perspectives, measurements, and evaluations.

NOTE

1. Address by Daniel P. Moynihan, Arthur K. Solomon lecture, New York University School of Business, April 29, 1971, p. 43.

BIBLIOGRAPHY

Abt, Clark C. *The Social Audit for Management.* New York: Amacom, 1977.

Ackerman, Robert W. *The Social Challenge to Business.* Cambridge, Mass.: Harvard University Press, 1976.

Ackerman, Robert W., and Raymond Bauer. *Corporate Social Responsiveness: The Modern Dilemma.* Reston, Va.: Reston Publishing, 1976.

Alexander, Michael O., and J. Leslie Livingstone. "What Are the Real Costs and Benefits of Producing 'Clean' Electric Power?" *Public Utilities Fortnightly*, August 30, 1973.

"Auto Makers Play an Expensive New Game." *Business Week*, October 27, 1977.

Barnett, A. H. "Accounting for Corporate Social Performance: A Survey." *Management Accounting*, November 1974.

Bauer, Raymond. "The Future of Corporate Social Accounting." In *Corporate Social Accounting*, edited by Meinholf Dierkes and Raymond Bauer. New York: Praeger, 1973.

Bauer, Raymond, L. Terry Canthorn, and Ronne P. Warner. "Auditing the Management Process for Social Performance." *Business and Society Review*, Fall 1975.

Bauer, Raymond, and Dan H. Fenn, Jr. *The Corporate Social Audit.* New York: Amacom, 1977.

Beams, Floyd, and Paul E. Fertig. "Pollution Control through Social Cost Conversion." *Journal of Accountancy*, November 1971.

Beresford, Dennis R. "Social Responsibility Disclosure Grows." *Management Accounting*, May 1977.

Beresford, Dennis R., and Stewart A. Feldman. "Companies Increase Social Responsibility Disclosure." *Management Accounting*, March 1976.

Berliner, Joseph S. *Economy, Society and Welfare: A Study in Social Economics.* New York: Praeger, 1972.

Biderman, Albert D., and Thomas F. Drury. *Measuring Work Quality for Social Reporting.* New York: Wiley, 1976.

Blumberg, Phillip I. "The Public's 'Right to Know': Disclosure in the Major American Corporation." *The Business Lawyer*, July 1973.

Bowen, Howard R. *Social Responsibilities of the Businessman.* New York: Harper & Row, 1953.

Bowman, Edward, and Mason Haire. "A Strategic Posture toward Corporate Social Reporting." *California Management Review,* Winter 1975.

Brandon, C. H., and J. P. Matoney, Jr. "Social Responsibility Financial Statement." *Management Accounting,* November 1975.

Butcher, Bernard. "An Anatomy of a Social Performance Report." *Business and Society Review,* Autumn 1973.

Carroll, Archie B., and George W. Beiler. "Landmarks in the Evolution of Social Audit." *Academy of Management Journal,* September 1975.

Cassell, Frank H. "The Social Cost of Doing Business." *MSU Business Topics,* Autumn 1974.

Charnes, A., Claude S. Colantoni, and W. W. Cooper. "Economic, Social and Enterprise Accounting and Mathematical Models." In *Accounting for Social Goals: Budgeting and Analysis of Non-Market Projects,* edited by J. Leslie Livingstone and S. C. Gunn. New York: Harper & Row, 1974.

Charnes, A., W. W. Cooper, and George Kozmetsky. "Measuring, Monitoring and Modeling Quality of Life." *Management Science,* June 1973.

Churchill, Neil C., and John K. Shank. "Accounting for Affirmative Action Programs: A Stochastic Flow Approach." *The Accounting Review,* October 1975.

——. "Affirmative Action and Quilt-Edged Goals." *Harvard Business Review,* March-April 1976.

Colantoni, Claude S., W. W. Cooper, and H. J. Dietzer. "Accounting and Social Reporting." In *Objectives of Financial Statements,* edited by Joe Cramer and George Sorter. New York: American Institute of CPA, 1974.

——. Budgeting Disclosure and Social Accounting." In *Corporate Social Accounting,* edited by Meinholf Dierkes and Raymond Bauer. New York: Praeger, 1973.

Committee on Social Measurement. *The Measurement of Corporate Social Performance.* New York: American Institute of CPA, 1977.

"Corporate Clout for Consumers." *Business Week,* September 12, 1977.

Corson, John J., and George A. Steiner. *Measuring Business's Social Performance: The Corporate Social Audit.* New York: Committee for Economic Development, 1974.

Dierkes, Meinholf, and Raymond Bauer. *Corporate Social Accounting.* New York: Praeger, 1973.

Dilley, Steven C. "External Report of Social Responsibility." *MSU Business Topics,* Autumn 1975.

Dilley, Steven C., and Jerry J. Weygandt. "Measuring Social Responsibility: An Empirical Test." *Journal of Accounting,* September 1973.

Eibert, Henry, and I. Robert Parket. "The Current Status of Corporate Social Responsibility." *Business Horizons,* August 1973.

Elias, Nabil, and Marc Epstein. "Dimensions of Corporate Social Reporting." *Management Accounting,* March 1975.

Epstein, Marc, et al. *Corporate Social Performance: The Measurement of Product and Service Contributions.* New York: National Association of Accountants, 1977.

Estes, Ralph. *Corporate Social Accounting.* New York: Wiley Interscience, 1976.

——. "Standards for Corporate Social Reporting." *Management Accounting,* November 1976.

Fair Employment Practices. Washington, D.C.: Bureau of National Affairs, 1976.

Frederick, William, and David H. Blake. *Social Auditing.* New York: Praeger, 1977.

Gray, Daniel. "One Way to Go about Inventing Social Accounting." In *Corporate Social Accounting,* edited by Meinholf Dierkes and Raymond Bauer. New York: Praeger, 1973.

Hay, R. H. "Social Auditing: An Experimental Approach." *Academy of Management Journal,* December 1975.

Hetland, James L., Jr. "The Social Audit: First National Bank's Experience." Address before the American Bankers Association, 1974 Public Affairs Conference, February 11, 1974.

Higgins, James M. "A Proposed Social Performance Evaluation System." *Atlanta Economic Review,* May-June 1977.

Johnson, Harold L. *Business in Contemporary Society: Framework and Issues.* Belmont, Calif.: Wadsworth, 1971.

Keller, Wayne. "Accounting for Corporate Social Performance." *Management Accounting,* February 1974.

"L'Examen social 1976 des entreprise Moyennes." *L'Expansion,* April 1976.

Linowes, David. *The Corporate Conscience.* New York: Hawthorne Books, 1974.

——. *Strategies for Survival.* New York: Amacom, 1973.

Mason, Edward S., ed. *The Large Corporation in Modern Society.* Cambridge, Mass.: Harvard University Press, 1960.

McAdam, Terry W. "How to Put Corporate Responsibility into Practice." *Business and Society/Innovation,* Summer 1973.

Moynihan, Daniel P. Arthur K. Solomon Lecture, New York University School of Business, April 29, 1971.

Nordhaus, William, and James Tobin. "Is Growth Obsolete?" *Economic Research: Retrospect and Prospect*, 50th Anniversary Colloquium 5. New York: National Bureau of Economic Research, 1972.

Panord, W. C., and W. P. Salzarulo. "Social Auditing: A Footnote of Full Disclosure." *Intellect*, November 1974.

Parsons, Talcott, and Neil J. Smelser. *Economy and Society: A Study in the Integration of Economic and Social Theory*. New York: Free Press, 1956.

Preston, Lee E., and James E. Post. *Private Management and Public Policy: The Principle of Public Responsibility*. Englewood Cliffs, N.J.: Prentice-Hall, 1975.

Purcell, Theodore V. "How G.E. Measures Managers in Fair Employment." *Harvard Business Review*, November-December 1974.

Ronen, Joshua. "Accounting for Social Costs and Benefits." In *Objectives of Financial Statements*, edited by Joe. S. Cramer and George Sorter. New York: American Institute of CPA, 1974.

Ruder, David S. "Public Obligations of Private Corporations." *University of Pennsylvania Law Review*, 1965.

Samuelson, Paul E. *Economics*. New York: McGraw-Hill, 1973.

Sater, Clair. *Corporate Rating Project, Final Report. Committee for Corporate Responsibility*. Palo Alto, Calif.: Stanford Graduate School of Business, December 1971.

Schaffer, Dick. "Time to Jot up a Social Audit." *The Accountant's Digest*, March 1976.

Schoebaum, Thomas J. "The Relationship between Corporate Disclosure and Corporate Responsibility." *Fordham Law Review*, 1972.

Schwartz, Donald E. "Corporate Responsibility in the Age of Aquarius." *The Business Lawyer*, November 1970.

Schwartz, R. A. "Corporate Philanthropic Contributions." *Journal of Finance*, June 1968.

Seidler, Lee J., and Lynn Seidler. *Social Accounting: Theory and Issues and Cases*. Los Angeles: Melville Publishing, 1975.

Shocker, Allan D., and S. Prakash Sethi. "An Approach to Incorporating Social Preferences in Developing Corporate Action Strategies." In *The Unstable Ground: Corporate Social Policy in a Dynamic Society*, edited by S. Prakash Sethi. Los Angeles: Melville Publishing, 1974.

Shulman, James, and Jeffrey Gale. "Laying the Groundwork for Social Accounting." *Financial Executive*, March 1972.

Social Indicators. Executive Office of the President, Office of Management and Budget, 1973.

Stone, Christopher D. *Where the Law Ends: The Social Control of Corporate Behavior.* New York: Harper Colophon Books, 1975.

Strawser, Robert H., Keith G. Stranga, and James J. Benjamin. "Social Reporting: Financial Community Views." *CPA Journal*, February 1976.

Sturdivant, Frederick D. *Business and Society: A Managerial Approach.* Homewood, Ill.: Richard D. Irwin, 1977.

Sturdivant, Frederick D., and James L. Ginter. "Corporate Social Responsiveness: Management Attitudes and Economic Performance." *California Management Review,* Spring 1977.

Tepper, John, et al. "Is Pollution Profitable?" *Risk Management,* April 1972.

Toan, Arthur, B., Jr. *The Measurement of Corporate Social Performance.* New York: American Institute of CPA, 1977.

Toward a Social Report, HEW, 1969.

INDEX

ABOUT THE AUTHOR

Harold L. Johnson is Professor of Economics, Graduate School of Business Administration, Emory University, Atlanta, Georgia. He holds a Ph.D. in Economics from the University of Texas (1952). He has been working in the area of Business and Society since 1957, teaching in the field since the early 1960s. Professor Johnson has written many articles on Business and Society, published in such journals as the *Harvard Business Review, Journal of Business, Southern Economic Journal, Behavioral Science, California Management Review,* and *Annals.* He is also the author of *Business in Contemporary Society: Framework and Issues.*

RELATED TITLES
Published by
Praeger Special Studies

Accounting and Reporting Practices of Private Foundations: A Critical Evaluation

Jack Traub

An Examination of Questionable Payments and Practices

Tom Kennedy and Charles E. Simon

*Social Auditing: Evaluating the Impact of Corporate Programs

David H. Blake, William C. Frederick, and Mildred S. Myers

*Also available in paperback.